APPLETON-CENTURY PHILOSOPHY SOURCE-BOOKS

STERLING P. LAMPRECHT, *Editor*

DE CIVE

OR

THE CITIZEN

APPLETON-CENTURY PHILOSOPHY
SOURCE-BOOKS

APPLETON-CENTURY PHILOSOPHY
SOURCE-BOOKS

St. Thomas Aquinas, *Concerning Being and Essence,* translated with a preface by George G. Leckie.

St. Aurelius Augustine, Bishop of Hippo, *Concerning the Teacher* and *On the Immortality of the Soul,* translated with a preface by George G. Leckie.

Thomas Hobbes, *De Cive* or *The Citizen,* edited with an introduction by Sterling P. Lamprecht.

Immanuel Kant, *The Fundamental Principles of the Metaphysic of Ethic,* translated with an introduction by Otto Manthey-Zorn.

John Locke, *Treatise of Civil Government* and *A Letter Concerning Toleration,* edited by Charles L. Sherman.

Benedict, de Spinoza, *Writings on Political Philosophy,* edited by A. G. A. Balz.

DE CIVE

OR

THE CITIZEN

BY

THOMAS HOBBES

Edited with An Introduction

by

STERLING P. LAMPRECHT
Professor of Philosophy, Amherst College

APPLETON-CENTURY-CROFTS

DIVISION OF MEREDITH CORPORATION

New York

PRINTED IN THE UNITED STATES OF AMERICA

E-44503

CONTENTS

things to be divided by lot. 18. The thirteenth, of birthright and first possession. 19. The fourteenth, of the safeguard of them who are mediators for peace. 20. The fifteenth, of constituting an umpire. 21. The sixteenth, that no man is judge in his own cause. 22. The seventeenth, that umpires must be without all hope of reward from those whose cause is to be judged. 23. The eighteenth, of witnesses. 24. The nineteenth, that there can no contract be made with the umpire. 25. The twentieth, against gluttony, and all such things as hinder the use of reason. 26. The rule by which we may presently know, whether what we are doing be against the law of nature or not. 27. The laws of nature oblige only in the court of conscience. 28. The laws of nature are sometimes broke by doing things agreeable to those laws. 29. The laws of nature are unchangeable. 30. Whosoever endeavors to fulfil the laws of nature, is a just man. 31. The natural and moral law are one. 32. How it comes to pass, that what hath been said of the laws of nature, is not the same with what philosophers have delivered concerning the virtues. 33. The law of nature is not properly a law, but as it is delivered in Holy Writ.

PART II. DOMINION

1. That the laws of nature are not sufficient to preserve peace. 2. That the laws of nature, in the state of nature, are silent. 3. That the security of living according to the laws of nature consists in the concord of many persons. 4. That the concord of many persons is not constant enough for a lasting peace. 5. The reason why the government of certain brute creatures stands firm in concord only, and why not of men. 6. That not only consent, but union also, is required to establish the peace of men. 7. What union is. 8. In union, the right of all men is conveyed to

their opinion who say that a lord with his servants
cannot make a city. 6. Exactions are more grievous
under a popular state than a monarchy. 7. Innocent
subjects are less exposed to penalties under a monarch than under the people. 8. The liberty of single
subjects is not less under a monarch than under a
people. 9. It is no disadvantage to the subjects, that
they are not all admitted to public deliberations.
10. Civil deliberations are unadvisedly committed to
great assemblies, by reason of the unskilfulness of
the most part of men. 11. In regard of eloquence. 12.
In regard of faction. 13. In regard of the unstableness
of the laws. 14. In regard of the want of secrecy. 15.
That these inconveniences adhere to democracy, forasmuch as men are naturally delighted with the
esteem of wit. 16. The inconveniences of a city arising from a king that is a child. 17. The power of
generals is an evident sign of the excellence of monarchy. 18. The best state of a city is that where the
subjects are the ruler's inheritance. 19. The nearer
aristocracy draws to monarchy, the better it is; the
further it keeps from it, the worse.

1. That the judging of good and evil belongs to private persons, is a seditious opinion. 2. That subjects
do sin by obeying their princes, is a seditious opinion.
3. That tyrannicide is lawful, is a seditious opinion.
4. That those who have the supreme power are subject to the civil laws, is a seditious opinion. 5. That
the supreme power may be divided, is a seditious
opinion. 6. That faith and sanctity are not acquired
by study and reason, but always supernaturally infused and inspired, is a seditious opinion. 7. That
each subject hath a propriety or absolute dominion
of his own goods, is a seditious opinion. 8. Not to
understand the difference between the people and the
multitude, prepares toward sedition. 9. Too great a
tax of monies, though never so just and necessary,

PART III. RELIGION

INTRODUCTION

THOMAS HOBBES was born near Malmesbury in Wiltshire, England, on April 5, 1588. His mother gave birth to him prematurely, as the story was told, because she took fright at the approach of the Spanish Armada to the English coast. He commented, late in life, on the circumstances of his birth in the words: "she brought forth twins—myself and fear." His remark has at least some purport. It reflects the realization of an old man of more than eighty years of age, that he had sought through a long life to make himself secure amidst the turmoils of civil war and violent shifts of political power. It also indicates a fundamental theme of his political philosophy, namely, that the prime need of man, a need which must be satisfied before any other consequent goods may be obtained, is peace under a stable government.

Hobbes was given educational opportunities through the beneficence of an uncle. He was taught Greek and Latin as a boy, and was sent to Oxford where he studied the writings of Aristotle, by whom, though he never acknowledged his indebtedness, he was obviously deeply influenced. Upon leaving Oxford in 1608, he became companion to a son of Lord Cavendish (who was later made Earl of Devonshire). And for the remaining seventy years of his long life, he continued in close contact with the Cavendish family, living for many years as a beloved retainer in their household and dying in their service on December 4, 1679. He was buried in the parish church at Ault Hucknall near Mansfield. On the stone slab which covers his grave, his patrons of the Cavendish family had a Latin epitaph inscribed which described him as "a man of integrity, well known at home and abroad for his reputation of learning."

Hobbes was throughout his life a man of letters. His first published work was a translation of Thucydides (1629); and among his last works was a metrical translation of the poems of Homer (1673, 1676). He spent much time on mathematical problems, endeavoring to square the circle, and getting into none-too-creditable controversy with John Wallis and other professional mathematicians of his day. He was associated for a time with Francis Bacon, even translating some of Bacon's essays into Latin; but aside from the fact that he repeated (without acknowledgment) Bacon's famous aphorism "Knowledge is power," he seems to have taken little from Bacon. He was profoundly influenced by the thought of Galileo and aimed to make the laws of motion the foundation of an entire system of philosophy. He read Descartes (and probably dined with Descartes in Paris); and he was one of the group of distinguished European intellectuals who read Descartes's *Meditations* in manuscript and wrote "objections" which Descartes published, with his answers, as an appendix to his work. Descartes did not have high regard for Hobbes's ideas on metaphysics; but Descartes said, after reading Hobbes's *De Cive,* that Hobbes was the soundest political thinker of the time. But all these multifarious literary and intellectual achievements of Hobbes are overshadowed by his chief contribution to the history of philosophy, that is, by his system of social and political philosophy.

The principles of this social and political philosophy came to development in Hobbes's mind through his reflections on the actual course of human affairs in the troubled world of the seventeenth century. It is indeed true, and it has often been pointed out (usually in disparagement of Hobbes), that Hobbes conceived these principles as part of a grandiose schematism for a total theory of the universe. According to this schematism, the only ultimate facts are matter and motion; all else is but some special case of the basic realities of matter and motion. The schematism would, Hobbes thought, have three main parts: a theory of body in general, a theory of living body (particularly of man), and a theory of social body (that is, of the state). Hobbes wrote eventually all three parts of this inclusive schematism: *De Corpore* (1655), *De Homine* (1650), and *De Cive* (1642). But he wrote the last part first; and internal evidence makes it highly probable that he in no sense deduced his political principles from the general materialistic schematism. He outlined the three parts of his schematism in "The Author's Preface to the Reader" of the *De Cive,* and he is known to have had it in mind even earlier. But the principles are the work of a fresh, realistic, empirical, sensitive observer of events. Hobbes's mind was prepared by his reading of Aristotle and Thucydides and other such attentive critics of the human scene; but his writing shows that he kept his eyes directly upon men's actions. He witnessed the strife which led up to the deposition and execution of Charles I, the fighting of the civil wars under Cromwell, the confusion after Cromwell's death, the Restoration under Charles II, and the constant struggle for power which continued between king and Parliament and among the various religious groups in England. His political principles were formulated long before the end of this sequence of events, and were only intensified and made more extreme by the later events. His principles were clear in his own mind when, late in 1640, he fled to France to escape the storm which was breaking with violence upon his own country, for by 1640 he had composed a sketch of his political theories in *The Elements of Law Natural and Politic* (though he chose never to publish this preliminary work). Then in 1642 he completed the *De Cive* which gave

classic form to his principles. The years of exile in France
(where he remained eleven years) added venom to his views
of the relation of civil government and religious institutions.
He acquired personal reasons for hating ecclesiastics. For after
Charles, Prince of Wales, arrived in Paris in 1646, Hobbes
secured appointment to tutor the prince in mathematics, but
lost the position because the ecclesiastics about Charles were
venomously hostile to Hobbes's frankly secular ideas of government. When he again expressed his political principles in
the *Leviathan* in 1651, he accompanied them with a furious
denunciation of the Church of Rome and Presbyterian clergy
and all who would make religion superior to or even independent of governmental control. Though the later work thus
puts Hobbes's political principles in a new (and not helpful)
context, the principles remain exactly what they were in 1640
and 1642.

The *De Cive* was Hobbes's earliest published work on social and political philosophy. When it appeared at Paris in
1642, it was in the form of a privately printed book, of which
few copies were made and very few have survived to our day.
It became available to those who wished to buy it through
three distinct editions published by the Elzevir Press of Am-
sterdam in 1647. An English translation appeared at London
in 1651. Hobbes was himself the translator of the *De Cive,* so
that the English text here given has equal authority with that
of the original Latin. When he translated the *De Cive* into
English, he gave it a long and cumbersome title which is
printed in full at the close of this introduction. In this edition,
the work is called simply, *The Citizen.*

The Citizen is not merely Hobbes's earliest published work
on social and political philosophy: it is also, in certain respects,
his best work. It far surpasses in clarity the preliminary sketch
of 1640 and the *De Corpore Politico* of 1650 which is nothing

more than certain chapters out of the early sketch. It has been comparatively neglected, however, because of the far greater fame of the longer work, the *Leviathan,* of 1651. The *Leviathan* was written by Hobbes directly in English (though put by him into Latin in 1668), and has not some of the unfortunate Latinisms which characterize the English text of *The Citizen.* As a contribution to *belles lettres,* the *Leviathan* ranks far ahead of *The Citizen.* In suitability of style to content and in vigor of trenchant and dramatic utterance, the *Leviathan* is one of the masterpieces of English literature. Yet, eloquent as it is when taken paragraph by paragraph, quotable as it is when taken sentence by sentence, it bears many marks of having been composed in the heat of bitter controversy. It was written when Hobbes, dismissed from service to Prince Charles and fearful of the conspiracies of prelates against him, decided to flee from France as no longer a safe residence and to make peace with Cromwell and so to return home. Begun in a spirit of moderation, it passes in its middle chapters to passionate rhetoric, and closes in a burst of fury against the religious forces which Hobbes characterizes as "The Kingdom of Darkness." It lacks the reasoned integrity and scholarly poise and philosophical objectivity of *The Citizen. The Citizen* indicates by its divisions the essential course of Hobbes's systematic thought; the *Leviathan* indicates rather the intensity of his hates. *The Citizen* is more methodical and more direct in exposition of Hobbes's constructive ideas and purpose; the *Leviathan* often distorts these ideas and obscures this purpose by an insistent fire of destructive attacks. Much of the *Leviathan,* because it was directed against factors that no longer loom up as menacingly as in Hobbes's day, is outmoded. *The Citizen,* free from all traces of personal animus, remains a definitive statement of one of the great interpretations of the social and political life of mankind.

Hobbes's political philosophy was greeted in his own day by
a more extensive and more virulent rejection than, probably,
any other philosophy in modern times. Many of the pamphlets
and broadsides directed at Hobbes have doubtless perished. But
we can name fifty-one hostile criticisms which were printed
against Hobbes during his lifetime and the next ensuing
decade, and we know of only two defenses of him (both of
which were composed by continental authors)! The almost
universal storm of fury against Hobbes's political ideas began to create in England, from the very outset of their first
publication in *The Citizen,* a myth concerning the intent and
purport of Hobbes's philosophy. Hobbes's works were more
denounced than read, as the nature of many of the attacks indicates. Hobbes was called "the monster of Malmesbury," and
was classified as an atheist, a schemer, a heretic, and a blas-
phemer. The House of Commons considered the advisability
of having a public burning of Hobbes's books, and some
bishops of the Church of England recommended the burning
of Hobbes's person. Whenever any one was greatly disliked,
he was likely to be called "a Hobbist"—no more objectionable
term of abuse could be found!

Hobbism, therefore, is not a name for the philosophy of
Hobbes. It designates that system or jumble of political notions
which the contemporary literature against Hobbes attributed to
him. Hobbism is derived from the writings of Hobbes by
wresting phrases out of context, by failing to note definitions
of terms and to draw distinctions which Hobbes clearly gives,
and by taking Hobbes's recognition of the evil in the world
around us as evidence of Hobbes's own sordidness of character.
The curious thing about this myth of Hobbism is that it (like
the age-old misrepresentation of Epicureanism) has survived
across the centuries and is repeated, more or less innocently, in
textbooks and histories today. No clearer way of expounding

the political principles of Hobbes can be found than to con-
trast it, point by point, with what may be called Hobbism.

1. According to Hobbism, God made man such a beast and
a rascal that he inclines universally to malice and fraud. Man's
typical acts, unless he is restrained by force, are violent and
ruthless, savagely disregarding the persons and property of his
fellows. His greatest longing is to preserve himself by gaining
power over others and exploiting others for his own egoistic
ends. And the exercise of power is honorable, no matter for
what ends it be exercised.

In his view of human nature, Hobbes is far from being a
Hobbist. He gave, to be sure, a picture of "man in the state
of nature" which is far from flattering. "All men in the state
of nature have a desire and will to hurt" (I, 4).* "The natural
state of men" is "a war of all men against all men" (I, 12).
But Hobbes did not intend to say that his picture of men in
the state of nature is a complete account of human nature. The
state of nature is for Hobbes, not an historical, but an analytical
concept. It is not some early stage of human existence from
which men later departed: it is rather a permanent factor
within all human societies against which men must always be
on their guard in practice and of which social theory must
take full account. The "natural man" is what man would become whenever he came wholly under the domination of passion, without the restraints of reason or of the established
procedures of civil society. The idea of man in the state of
nature is for social science like that of a natural body in
physical science. Physical science holds that a body continues
in a state of rest or of uniform motion in a straight line unless
influenced by outside forces. Actually, there is no body which
is not influenced by outside bodies; but the idea of such a body

---

* All references, unless specifically noted, are to chapter and article of
The Citizen.

enables us to measure the outside forces. So the concept of man in the state of nature enables us to measure the extent to which reason and social pressures qualify the expression of human passions. It makes evident the gravity of the problem of securing a stable, and even moderately decent, civil society.

The men we have actually to deal with are neither pure samples of natural men nor clear embodiments of virtue. They exhibit varying degrees of crudity and refinement. Men are not, Hobbes explicitly stated, naturally evil (Preface to the Reader). But they are naturally passionate. And their passions will make them evil in some conditions, and will lead them to vigorous support of desirable social ends in other conditions. One can not persuade water to run uphill, but one may pump it some distance upwards. So one can not persuade men to be passionless; but one may so organize a state that men will gratify their passions within the definable limits of civilized ways. In brief, excellence comes, if it come at all, not from romantic trust in human nature, but from realistic knowledge of what the forces are which require control. Man is a rational as well as a passionate animal. But human reason is impotent to control passion unless and until social conditions are established which are conducive to the profitable exercise of reason.

2. According to the system we are calling Hobbism, there is no genuine distinction between right and wrong. Moral distinctions are artificial suppositions foisted upon the generality of mankind by some superior power; they are arbitrary conventions which rulers impose upon their subjects and have no validity beyond the frontiers within which those rulers exercise control. All morality is thus a fiat morality. The state is the creator of what men have come to deem virtue, and apart from the state there would be no moral distinctions or moral principles at all.

Readers of Hobbes will find many passages which, pried from context, seem to maintain what Hobbism thus asserts. For example:

In the state of nature, to have all, and to do all, is lawful for all; and this is that which is meant by that coming saying, nature hath given all to all, from whence we understand likewise, that in the state of nature, profit is the measure of right (X, 10).

Before there was any government, just and unjust had no being, their nature only being relative to some command, and every action in its own nature is indifferent; that it becomes just or unjust, proceeds from the right of the magistrate (XII, 1).

These passages quoted from Hobbes's *The Citizen* and many other passages in his various writings have often misled his readers. Properly understood, however, they do not imply Hobbism. Two things need to be said in order to establish a correct interpretation of Hobbes's meaning. First, Hobbes is speaking in legal, not in moral, terms. Justice and right are being defined in terms of enforcement of a conformity to law. It is then an analytical proposition and admits of no dispute that where there is no law there can be no question of justice or right at all. Justice then begins only where law exists. And in the absence of law, might makes right, not in the sense that might proves wisdom or virtue to be resident in him who exercises that might, but in the sense that might, when irresistible, is the beginning of a régime in which the distinction between social requirements and individual interest is emerging, in which, hence, the force of law is beginning to manifest itself and respect for law is involved in the determination of conduct.

Secondly, Hobbes is insisting that any significant morality is social in character and presupposes the occurrence of regularized procedures. Morality is not significantly present when men are considered in their separateness as atomic individuals; it is significantly present when men are considered in their interrelations in situations which call for social adjustments. If a critic wishes to press Hobbes by claiming that a man, apart from his fellows, can yet live on a morally higher or lower scale, Hobbes will grant the point. He did indeed grant it, when in the Elzevir editions of *The Citizen* he printed footnotes that were not in the Paris edition of 1642 (cf. footnote to III, 27). Drunkenness, cruelty, and revenge which respects not the future good, are, he explicitly affirmed, evil even in the state of war (and the state of war is the irruption of the state of nature). There is then the beginning of morality apart from social institutions; but the big and important concerns of morality arise only in developed societies and in the context of social institutions of many kinds.

Hobbes never maintained, as Hobbism attributed to him, that law creates moral distinctions by fiat. His point was that, precisely because justice and right have important meanings as legal terms, morality must be viewed as a genuinely social affair. If men lived without a known law and a civil power to enforce it, they would have no guide except their individual judgments; consequently, opinions would clash, strife would ensue, and chaos would result. To recognize this fact is not to endorse ruthless, anti-social, and passionate acts: it is rather to indicate the indispensable rôle of law in pursuit of the good life. If one supposed that individual men in their individuality were so many separate seats of moral prerogatives and moral obligations, then one would have to go on to view morality as fixed antecedently to the enactment of laws, and to regard it the function of lawmakers merely to frame laws consistent with this fixed and antecedent standard. Such a position would be a superficial notion of the intimate involvement of law and morals in each other. Law, as Hobbes saw, creates situations

in which sound reason or sound moral principle (two names
for the same thing) requires decisions such as would be ridiculous if there were no law or if there were a different law.
Law does not by fiat create moral distinctions, and Hobbes
never said it does. But law does create significant moral situations, and Hobbes saw this point more clearly than any prior
political philosopher of modern times.

3. A third point of Hobbism followed naturally from the
second. It was that a *de facto* ruler is always justified in all
his laws and acts. Since the distinction between good and bad
arises from the dictate of princes, the commands of princes
are *ipso facto* the criterion of right and wrong for those whom
they are strong enough to command. A bad lawmaker is thus
a contradiction in terms; for being himself the source of
morality, he can not be immoral.

Here again, there are passages in Hobbes which, at first
glance, seem to be Hobbist. For example:

Legitimate kings therefore make the things they command just,
by commanding them, and those which they forbid, unjust, by
forbidding them (XII, 1).

It belongs to the same chief power to make some common rules
for all men, and to declare them publicly, by which every man
may know what may be called his, what another's, what just,
what unjust, what honest, what dishonest, what good, what evil
(VI, 9).

There are no authentical doctrines concerning right and wrong,
good and evil, besides the constituted laws in each realm and government (The Preface to the Reader).

These are strong words, and doubtless there is overstatement
in them. But it should be remembered that Hobbes is using
his terms in their legal sense. His intent is to show that the
source of law can hardly be contrary to law; that, if we are to

bar a resort to violence and war, sovereign power must rest somewhere; that civil society carries with it the obligation to respect law as such. Even bad law is law, and even good citizens can not properly flout bad law as if it were not really law at all. Since law establishes, in part at least, the situations which define our moral problems, it can not, in any competent and incisive moral conduct, be treated as either inconsequential or irrelevant. He who ignores the legal purport of his acts destroys *ipso facto* the moral legitimacy of those acts.

Hobbes repudiated in all his writings the Hobbist contention that the king can do no wrong. He had much to say "concerning the duties of them who bear rule," to quote the title of Chapter XIII. Though a sovereign can not, by legal definition, act unjustly, he "may diverse ways transgress against the other laws of nature, as by cruelty, iniquity, contumely, and other like vices" (VII, 14). A sovereign, as much as any other man, is subject to the laws of nature or the dictates of reason; indeed he has greater responsibility to those laws than other men because he is by function the person in whose hands social welfare is placed. "The safety of the people is the supreme law" (XIII, 2). "The city was not instituted for its own, but for the subjects' sake" (XIII, 3). Good government involves provisions to increase the number of the people, to preserve peace at home, to provide defense against attack from without, and generally to safeguard "the commodity of living." And by commodity of living Hobbes meant such regulations as will give encouragement to trade, abundant opportunity for labor, ample supplies of food and other necessities, and such liberty of movement and of private affairs as is compatible with maintenance of public order. Not simply may a sovereign violate his responsibilities to his people through indulgence in vice or through neglect, but even a conscientious sovereign may commit such vital mistakes of judgment that his rule involves serious moral disasters. All this Hobbes re-iterated so often that his theory stands in strong antithesis to the notion of Hobbism.

4. A fourth point of Hobbism is the denial of all rights to the people, and the assertion that the passing whims of a ruler are of more force than what is alleged to be law.

Hobbes came closer to being a Hobbist on this point than on any other. His words are indeed austere. "Whatsoever shall be done by him who commands, must not be punished" (VI, 12). Or, in the words of the *Leviathan*: "The sovereign power ... implieth an universal impunity" (Molesworth edition of *The English Works*, Vol. III, p. 205). But Hobbes's point was not that men in civil society do not have certain specific rights as defined and established by law; it was that these rights are historically conditioned and can not be taken as common to all systems of law, much less as inhering in men apart from laws altogether.

Hobbes was here an effective realist. He discerned clearly that common agreement among men could not be expected on all issues and at all times, and that, consequently, and if civil war is to be avoided, some one, somewhere, must be given sovereign power to settle conflicting issues. In such cases, men have to choose between open strife and imposed settlement. Wise rulers and prudent citizens will seek to prevent occasions of irreconcilable and embittered opposition. But a great aid in preventing such occasions and in producing mutual com-promise of conflicting claims, is the existence of a power which contending factions know to be ready to step in and compel peace.

Furthermore, as Hobbes saw, the appeal to popular rights can be a technique of obstructing needed social change. Appeal from sovereign power to alleged rights is virtually appeal from a present sovereign to a dead sovereign whose power established those rights. No one ever saw more clearly than Hobbes the importance of law; but also no one ever saw more clearly than Hobbes that no force in human society is more human in its origins than law, more experimental in its course, more tentative in its objectives, more dependent in its specific meanings upon the authorities who use and interpret it. The nature of property rights and of the rights of labor have been changing rapidly in our own country during recent decades; and the appeal to fixed rights has been a technique of reactionaries who sought to prevent change. Even the rights assigned to the people by "the bill of rights" in the first ten amendments to the Constitution of the United States, even these rights are subject to change by the amending powers which the Constitution confers on the sovereign people; and regard for these rights is, not so much an appeal to unchangeable law, as a program of action and an act of faith. The "four freedoms" of the Atlantic Charter are certainly contingent upon establishment of governments which will bring them to factual realization instead of leaving them to pious wishes. And so Hobbes was right in recognizing sovereign power as the creator of rights rather than as conditioned in its power by antecedent rights. Legalism ties a society to precedent, to the level of past achievement. Hobbes's appeal to sovereignty, with all the faults of its tendency to harsh overstatement, is in theory a release from outworn precedent. It is in theory a turning from precedents to the ultimate source of law, in the interest of securing better and more pertinent law.

There yet remains something ruthless in Hobbes's words that sovereign power implies universal impunity, something ruthless which, if not justifying an interpretation of him as a Hobbist, yet calls for careful consideration. Hobbes put his sovereign not merely above law but above criticism. In the closing chapter of *The Citizen,* the ruthlessness of Hobbes's theory comes out glaringly. Not simply in matters temporal, but in matters spiritual, that is, in matters of religious conviction and of conscience, a citizen is bound, Hobbes wrote, dutifully to obey his sovereign. And there is no proper alternative to this submission, Hobbes continued, except to "go to Christ by martyrdom" (XVIII, 13). That is, a citizen must obey or die: he must not criticise and expect to be tolerated and to be allowed to survive.

And exactly here is to be found a major fault in Hobbes. Hobbes's appeal to force was insistent because his distrust of human reason was excessive. He did not deny the power of reason to discern the laws of natue which are the principles of right reasoning and the laws of sound morality; but he did deny that men are intelligent enough to follow the paths of reasonableness. And because men are not sufficiently reasonable (a fact which can be abundantly confirmed empirically), Hobbes refused any proper play to reason in human affairs. Hobbes had no sense for what Englishmen call "His Majesty's Loyal Opposition." He had no sense for either the privilege or the duty of a sovereign to provide for criticism, to promote the free exchange and discussion of ideas in order that policy be clarified and purposes be enlightened. Hobbes treated reasoning as sedition against authority, criticism as treason, discussion of policy as a mark of the dissolution of commonwealth. He seems to have supported the notion that strong government is one under which reasoning and criticism and discussion are not visible.

The historian may explain this element of ruthlessness in Hobbes by pointing to his fear of anarchy, his suffering from the general confusion of affairs in the seventeenth century, and his desire to get something settled with finality. But the critic must weigh the merits of what the historian explains. And the critic may well see in Hobbes's distrust of reason a danger which might dissolve Hobbes's sound principles into that very Hobbism which Hobbes did not espouse. For if reason be effete and impotent, then the natural man tends to become the entire man, moral distinctions tend to become arbitrary fiats, and any sovereign might be justified in all his ways. Had the opponents of Hobbes focused their attack upon his distrust of reason, they would have been able to make out a trenchant case. But of course they too distrusted reason, preferring to appeal to some principle of legitimacy, some ecclesiastical authoritarianism, some hereditary institution. Had Hobbes recognized the rôle that reason may play in human affairs, he would have preserved his social and political philosophy from the tinge of ruthlessness which now characterizes it. But even as it is, that philosophy is a monumental contribution to the thought of mankind and one of the few really definitive theories concerning the state and the citizen.

In the text of *The Citizen* which is here given, the spelling of Hobbes has been modernized, the punctuation has been somewhat altered to make it more helpful to the reader, most of the italics have been removed, and, occasionally, some long sentences have been broken up into two or more shorter ones. But the text is otherwise Hobbes's own English translation of *The Citizen* as he himself prepared it for publication in 1651. The text here given is much more faithful to the original of 1651 than is that of the Molesworth edition of 1841 which is the only edition of *The Citizen* which has been available to readers for more than a century.

STERLING P. LAMPRECHT

BIBLIOGRAPHY

Hobbes's Works, edited by Sir W. Molesworth, 11 volumes of the English Works, 5 volumes of the Latin Works, 1839-1845.

LAIRD, J.: *Hobbes*, London, 1934.

LAMPRECHT, S. P.: "Hobbes and Hobbism," in *The American Political Science Review*, Vol. XXXIV, no. 1, February, 1940, pp. 31-53. (I have used extensive portions of this article in preparing the introduction to this edition of *The Citizen*, and I wish to thank the editors of the *Review* for their kind permission to do so.)

LYON, G.: *La philosophie de Hobbes*, Paris, 1893.

ROBERTSON, G. C.: *Hobbes*, Edinburgh and Philadelphia, 1886.

STEPHEN, Sir L.: *Hobbes*, London and New York, 1904.

STRAUSS, L.: *The Political Philosophy of Hobbes: Its Basis and Its Genesis*. Translated from the German manuscript by E. M. Sinclair. Oxford, 1936.

TAYLOR, A. E.: *Thomas Hobbes*, New York, 1909, and London, 1908.

TAYLOR, A. E.: "The Ethical Doctrine of Hobbes," in *Philosophy*, Vol. XIII, October, 1938, pp. 406-424.

TÖNNIES, F.: *Thomas Hobbes, Leben und Lehre*, 3rd edition, Stuttgart, 1925.

WOODBRIDGE, F. J. E.: *Selections from Hobbes*, New York, 1930.

BIBLIOGRAPHY

Philosophical Rudiments

CONCERNING

GOVERNMENT and SOCIETY

or,

A DISSERTATION *concerning* MAN in his several
Habitudes and Respects, as the
Member of a SOCIETY, first
SECULAR, and then SACRED.

Containing

The ELEMENTS OF CIVIL POLITY in the
Agreement which it hath both
with NATURAL and DIVINE LAWS.

In which is demonstrated

Both what the ORIGIN OF JUSTICE is,
and wherein the ESSENCE OF CHRISTIAN
RELIGION doth consist.

Together with

The NATURE, LIMITS, and QUALIFICATIONS
both of REGIMENT and SUBJECTION.

By Tho. Hobbes

LONDON
Printed by J. G. for R. Royston,
at the Angel in Ivie-lane. 1651.

TO THE RIGHT HONOURABLE,

WILLIAM, EARL OF DEVONSHIRE,

MY MOST HONOURED LORD.

MAY IT PLEASE YOUR LORDSHIP,

IT was the speech of the Roman people (to whom the name
of king had been rendered odious, as well by the tyranny of the
Tarquins, as by the genius and decretals of that city) it was
the speech, I say, of the public, however pronounced from a
private mouth, (if yet Cato the censor were no more than
such) that all kings are to be reckoned amongst ravenous beasts.
But what a beast of prey was the Roman people, whilst with
its conquering eagles it erected its proud trophies so far and
wide over the world, bringing the Africans, the Asiatics, the
Macedonians, and the Achæans, with many other despoiled nations, into a specious bondage, with the pretence of preferring
them to be denizens of Rome? So that if Cato's saying were
a wise one, it was every whit as wise that of Pontius Telesinus;
who flying about with open mouth through all the companies
of his army, (in that famous encounter which he had with
Sylla) cried out, that Rome herself, as well as Sylla, was to
be razed; for that there would always be wolves and depreda-
tors of their liberty, unless the forest that lodged them were
grubbed up by the roots. To speak impartially, both sayings
are very true; that man to man is a kind of God; and that man
to man is an arrant wolf. The first is true, if we compare
citizens amongst themselves; and the second, if we compare
cities. In the one, there is some analogy of similitude with

the Deity, to wit, justice and charity, the twin sisters of peace. But in the other, good men must defend themselves by taking to them for a sanctuary the two daughters of war, deceit and violence: that is in plain terms a mere brutal rapacity: which although men object to one another as a reproach, by an inbred custom which they have of beholding their own actions in the persons of other men, wherein, as in a mirror, all things on the left side appear to be on the right, and all things on the right side to be as plainly on the left; yet the natural right of preservation which we all receive from the uncontrollable dictates of necessity, will not admit it to be a vice, though it confess it to be an unhappiness. Now that with Cato himself, (a person of so great a renown for wisdom) animosity should so prevail instead of judgment, and partiality instead of reason, that the very same thing which he thought equal in his popular state, he should censure as unjust in a monarchical, other men perhaps may have leisure to admire. But I have been long since of this opinion, that there was never yet any more-than-vulgar prudence, that had the luck of being acceptable to the giddy people; but either it hath not been understood, or else having been so, hath been levelled and cried down. The more eminent actions and apothegms both of the Greeks and Romans have been indebted for their eulogies not so much to the reason, as to the greatness of them, and very many times to that prosperous usurpation (with which our histories do so mutually upbraid each other) which as a conquering torrent carries all before it, as well public agents as public actions, in the stream of time. Wisdom properly so called is nothing else but this, the perfect knowledge of the truth in all matters whatsoever. Which being derived from the registers and records of things, and that as it were through the conduit of certain definite appellations, cannot possibly be the work of a sudden acuteness, but of a well-balanced reason, which by the compendium of a word, we call philosophy. For by this it is, that a way is opened to us, in which we travel from the contemplation of particular things to the inference or result of universal actions. Now look how many sorts of things there are which properly fall within the cognizance of human reason, into so many branches does the tree of philosophy divide itself. And from the diversity of the matter about which they are conversant, there hath been given to those branches a diversity of names too. For treating of figures, it is called geometry; of motion, physic; of natural right, morals; put all together, and they make up philosophy. Just as the British, the Atlantic, and the Indian seas, being diversely christened from the diversity of their shores, do notwithstanding all together make up the ocean. And truly the geometricians have very admirably performed their part. For whatsoever assistance doth accrue to the life of man, whether from the observation of the heavens, or from the description of the earth, from the notation of times, or from the remotest experiments of navigation; finally, whatsoever things they are in which this present age doth differ from the rude simpleness of antiquity, we must acknowledge to be a debt which we owe merely to geometry. If the moral philosophers had as happily discharged their duty, I know not what could have been added by human industry to the completion of that happiness, which is consistent with human life. For were the nature of human actions as distinctly known, as the nature of quantity in geometrical figures, the strength of avarice and ambition, which is sustained by the erroneous opinions of the vulgar, as touching the nature of right and wrong, would presently faint and languish; and mankind should enjoy such an immortal peace, that (unless it were for habitation, on supposition that the earth should grow too narrow for her inhabitants) there would hardly be left any pretence for war.

But now on the contrary, that neither the sword nor the pen should be allowed any cessation; that the knowledge of the law of nature should lose its growth, not advancing a whit beyond its ancient stature; that there should still be such siding with the several factions of philosophers, that the very same action should be decried by some, and as much elevated by others; that the very same man should at several times embrace his several opinions, and esteem his own actions far otherwise in himself than he does in others; these I say are so many signs, so many manifest arguments, that what hath hitherto been written by moral philosophers, hath not made any progress in the knowledge of the truth; but yet hath took with the world, not so much by giving any light to the understanding, as entertainment to the affections, whilst by the successful rhetorications of their speech they have confirmed them in their rashly received opinions. So that this part of philosophy hath suffered the same destiny with the public ways, which lie open to all passengers to traverse up and down, or the same lot with highways and open streets; some for divertisement, and some for business; so that what with the impertinences of some, and the altercations of others, those ways have never a seeds-time, and therefore yield never a harvest. The only reason of which unluckiness should seem to be this; that amongst all the writers of that part of philosophy, there is not one that hath used an idoneous principle of tractation. For we may not, as in a circle, begin the handling of a science from what point we please. There is a certain clue of reason, whose beginning is in the dark, but by the benefit of whose conduct, we are led as it were by the hand into the clearest light, so that the principle of tractation is to be taken from that darkness, and then the light to be carried thither for irradiating its doubts. As often therefore as any writer, doth either weakly forsake that clue, or wilfully cut it asunder, he describes the footsteps, not of his progress in science, but of his wanderings from it. And upon this it was, that when I applied my thoughts to the investigation of natural justice, I was presently advertised from the very word justice, (which signifies a steady will of giving every one his own) that my first enquiry was to be, from whence it proceeded, that any man should call anything rather his own, than another man's. And when I found that this proceeded not from nature, but consent, (for what nature at first laid forth in common, men did afterwards distribute into several impropriations), I was conducted from thence to another inquiry, namely to what end, and upon what impulsives, when all was equally every man's in common, men did rather think it fitting, that every man should have his inclosure. And I found the reason was, that from a community of goods, there must needs arise contention whose enjoyment should be greatest, and from that contention all kind of calamities must unavoidably ensue, which by the instinct of nature, every man is taught to shun. Having therefore thus arrived at two maxims of human nature, the one arising from the concupiscible part, which desires to appropriate to itself the use of those things in which all others have a joint interest, the other proceeding from the rational, which teaches every man to fly a contra-natural dissolution, as the greatest mischief that can arrive to nature; which principles being laid down, I seem from them to have demonstrated by a most evident connexion, in this little work of mine, first the absolute necessity of leagues and contracts, and thence the rudiments both of moral and of civil prudence. That appendage which is added concerning the regiment of God, hath been done with this intent, that the dictates of God Almighty in the law of nature, might not seem repugnant to the written law, revealed to us in his word. I have also been very wary in the whole tenour of my discourse, not to meddle with the civil laws of any particular nation whatsoever, that is to say, I have avoided coming ashore, which those times have so infested both with shelves and tempests. At what expense of time and industry I have been in this scrutiny after truth, I am not ignorant; but to what purpose, I know not. For being partial judges of ourselves, we lay a partial estimate upon our own productions. I therefore offer up this book to your Lordship's, not favour, but censure first; as having found by many experiments, that it is not the credit of the author, nor the newness of the work, nor yet the ornament of the style, but only the weight of reason, which recommends any opinion to your Lordship's favour and approbation. If it fortune to please, that is to say, if it be sound, if it be useful, if it be not vulgar; I humbly offer it to your Lordship as both my glory and my protection; but if in anything I have erred, your Lordship will yet accept it as a testimony of my gratitude, for that the means of study which I enjoyed by your Lordship's goodness, I have employed to the procurement of your Lordship's favour. The God of heaven crown your Lordship with length of days in this earthly station, and in the heavenly Jerusalem, with a crown of glory.

Your Honour's most humble,

and most devoted Servant,

THOMAS HOBBES.

THE AUTHOR'S

PREFACE TO THE READER

READER, I promise thee here such things, which ordinarily promised, do seem to challenge the greatest attention, and I lay them here before thine eyes, whether thou regard the dignity or profit of the matter treated of, or the right method of handling it, or the honest motive, and good advice to undertake it, or lastly the moderation of the author. In this book thou shalt find briefly described the duties of men, first as men; then as subjects, lastly, as Christians; under which duties are contained not only the elements of the laws of nature, and of nations, together with the true original and power of justice, but also the very essence of Christian religion itself, so far forth as the measure of this my purpose could well bear it.

Which kind of doctrine (excepting what relates to Christian religion) the most ancient sages did judge fittest to be delivered to posterity, either curiously adorned with verse, or clouded with allegories as a most beautiful and hallowed mystery of royal authority; lest by the disputations of private men it might be defiled. Other philosophers in the mean time, to the advantage of mankind, did contemplate the faces, and motions of things, others, without disadvantage, their natures and causes. But in after times, Socrates is said to have been the first, who truly loved this civil science, although hitherto not thoroughly understood, yet glimmering forth as through a cloud in the government of the commonweal, and that he set

7

so great a value on this, that utterly abandoning, and despising all other parts of philosophy, he wholly embraced this, as judging it only worthy the labour of his mind. After him comes Plato, Aristotle, Cicero, and other philosophers, as well Greek, as Latin. And now at length all men of all nations, not only philosophers, but even the vulgar, have and do still deal with this as a matter of ease, exposed and prostitute to every mother-wit, and to be attained without any great care or study. And, which makes mainly for its dignity, those who suppose themselves to have it, or are in such employment, as they ought to have it, do so wonderfully please themselves in its idea, as they easily brook the followers of other arts to be esteemed and styled ingenuous, learned, skilful, what you will; except prudent: for this name, in regard of civil knowledge, they presume to be due to themselves only. Whether therefore the worth of arts is to be weighed by the worthiness of the persons who entertain them, or by the number of those who have written of them, or by the judgment of the wisest; certainly this must carry it, which so nearly relates to princes, and others engaged in the government of mankind, in whose adulterate species also the most part of men do delight themselves, and in which the most excellent wits of philosophers have been conversant. The benefit of it when rightly delivered, that is, when derived from true principles by evident connection, we shall then best discern, when we shall but well have considered the mischiefs that have befallen mankind from its counterfeit and babbling form; for in such matters as are speculated for the exercise of our wits, if any error escape us, it is without hurt; neither is there any loss, but of time only: but in those things which every man ought to meditate for the steerage of his life, it necessarily happens, that not only from errors, but even from ignorance itself, there arise offences, contentions, nay even slaughter itself. Look now, how great a preju-

dice these are, such, and so great is the benefit arising from
this doctrine of morality truly declared. How many kings
(and those good men too) hath this one error, that a tyrant
king might lawfully be put to death, been the slaughter of?
How many throats hath this false position cut, that a prince
for some causes may by some certain men be deposed? And
what bloodshed hath not this erroneous doctrine caused, that
kings are not superiors to, but administrators for the multitude? Lastly, how many rebellions hath this opinion been the
cause of, which teacheth that the knowledge whether the commands of kings be just or unjust, belongs to private men, and
that before they yield obedience, they not only may, but ought
to dispute them? Besides, in the moral philosophy now commonly received, there are many things no less dangerous than
those, which it matters not now to recite. I suppose those ancients foresaw this, who rather chose to have the science of
justice wrapped up in fables, than openly exposed to disputations: for before such questions began to be moved, princes did
not sue for, but already exercised the supreme power. They
kept their empire entire, not by arguments, but by punishing
the wicked, and protecting the good. Likewise subjects did
not measure what was just by the sayings and judgments of
private men, but by the laws of the realm; nor were they kept
in peace by disputations, but by power and authority: yea, they
reverenced the supreme power, whether residing in one man
or in a council, as a certain visible divinity; therefore they little
used as in our days, to join themselves with ambitious, and
hellish spirits, to the utter ruin of their state; for they could
not entertain so strange a fancy as not to desire the preservation of that by which they were preserved. In truth, the sim-
plicity of those times was not yet capable of so learned a piece
of folly. Wherefore it was peace, and a golden age, which
ended not before that Saturn being expelled, it was taught

lawful to take up arms against kings. This I say, the ancients not only themselves saw, but in one of their fables, they seem very aptly to have signified it to us; for they say, that when Ixion was invited by Jupiter to a banquet, he fell in love, and began to court Juno herself; offering to embrace her, he clasped a cloud, from whence the Centaurs proceeded, by nature half men, half horses, a fierce, a fighting, and unquiet generation; which changing the names only, is as much as if they should have said, that private men being called to councils of state, desired to prostitute justice, the only sister and wife of the supreme, to their own judgments and apprehensions, but embracing a false and empty shadow instead of it, they have begotten those hermaphrodite opinions of moral philosophers, partly right and comely, partly brutal and wild, the causes of all contentions and bloodsheds. Since therefore such opinions are daily seen to arise, if any man now shall dispel those clouds, and by most firm reasons demonstrate that there are no authentical doctrines concerning right and wrong, good and evil, besides the constituted laws in each realm and government; and that the question whether any future action will prove just or unjust, good or ill, is to be demanded of none, but those to whom the supreme hath committed the interpretation of his laws; surely he will not only show us the highway to peace, but will also teach us how to avoid the close, dark, and dangerous by-paths of faction and sedition, than which I know not what can be thought more profitable.

Concerning my method, I thought it not sufficient to use a plain and evident style in what I have to deliver, except I took my beginning from the very matter of civil government, and thence proceeded to its generation, and form, and the first beginning of justice; for everything is best understood by its constitutive causes. For as in a watch, or some such small engine, the matter, figure, and motion of the wheels cannot well be known, except it be taken in sunder, and viewed in parts; so to make a more curious search into the rights of states, and duties of subjects, it is necessary, (I say not to take them in sunder, but yet that) they be so considered, as if they were dissolved, that is, that we rightly understand what the quality of human nature is, in what matters it is, in what not, fit to make up a civil government, and how men must be agreed amongst themselves, that intend to grow up into a well-grounded state. Having therefore followed this kind of method, in the first place I set down for a principle by experience known to all men, and denied by none, to wit, that the dispositions of men are naturally such, that except they be restrained through fear of some coercive power, every man will distrust and dread each other, and as by natural right he may, so by necessity he will be forced to make use of the strength he hath, toward the preservation of himself. You will object perhaps, that there are some who deny this; truly so it happens, that very many do deny it. But shall I therefore seem to fight against myself because I affirm that the same men confess, and deny the same thing? In truth I do not, but they do, whose actions disavow what their discourses approve of. We see all countries, though they be at peace with their neighbours, yet guarding their frontiers with armed men, their towns with walls and ports, and keeping constant watches. To what purpose is all this, if there be no fear of the neighbouring power? We see even in well-governed states, where there are laws and punishments appointed for offenders, yet particular men travel not without their sword by their sides, for their defences, neither sleep they without shutting not only their doors against their fellow subjects, but also their trunks and coffers for fear of domestics. Can men give a clearer testimony of the distrust they have each of other, and all, of all? How since they do thus, and even countries as well as men, they publicly profess their mutual fear and diffidence? But in disputing they deny it, that is as much as to say, that out of a desire they have to contradict others, they gainsay themselves. Some object that this principle being admitted, it would needs follow, not only that all men were wicked (which perhaps though it seem hard, yet we must yield to, since it is so clearly declared by holy writ) but also wicked by nature (which cannot be granted without impiety). But this, that men are evil by nature, follows not from this principle; for though the wicked were fewer than the righteous, yet because we cannot distinguish them, there is a necessity of suspecting, heeding, anticipating, sub-jugating, self-defending, ever incident to the most honest and fairest conditioned: much less does it follow that those who are wicked are so by nature, for though from nature, that is from their first birth, as they are merely sensible creatures, they have this disposition, that immediately as much as in them lies, they desire and do whatsoever is best pleasing to them, and that either through fear they fly from, or through hardness repel those dangers which approach them, yet are they not for this reason to be accounted wicked. For the affections of the mind which arise only from the lower parts of the soul are not wicked themselves, but the actions thence proceeding may be so sometimes, as when they are either offensive, or against duty. Unless you give children all they ask for, they are peevish, and cry, aye and strike their parents sometimes, and all this they have from nature, yet are they free from guilt, neither may we properly call them wicked; first, because they cannot hurt; next, because wanting the free use of reason they are exempted from all duty. These when they come to riper years, having acquired power whereby they may do hurt, if they shall con-tinue to do the same things, then truly they both begin to be, and are properly accounted wicked; in so much as a wicked man is almost the same thing with a child grown strong and sturdy, or a man of a childish disposition; and malice the same with a defect of reason in that age, when nature ought to be better governed through good education and experience. Unless therefore we will say that men are naturally evil, because they receive not their education and use of reason from nature, we must needs acknowledge that men may derive desire, fear, anger, and other passions from nature, and yet not impute the evil effects of those unto nature. The foundation therefore which I have laid standing firm, I demonstrate in the first place, that the state of men without civil society (which state we may properly call the state of nature) is nothing else but a mere war of all against all; and in that war all men have equal right unto all things; next, that all men as soon as they arrive to understanding of this hateful condition, do desire (even nature itself compelling them) to be freed from this misery. But that this cannot be done except by compact, they all quit that right they have to all things. Furthermore I declare, and confirm what the nature of compact is; how and by what means the right of one might be transferred unto another to make their compacts valid; also what rights, and to whom they must necessarily be granted for the establishing of peace, I mean what those dictates of reason are, which may properly be termed the laws of nature; and all these are contained in that part of this book which I entitle Liberty.

These grounds thus laid, I show further what civil government, and the supreme power in it, and the divers kinds of it are; by what means it becomes so, and what rights particular men, who intend to constitute this civil government, must so necessarily transfer from themselves on the supreme power, whether it be one man or an assembly of men, that except they do so it will evidently appear to be no civil government, but the rights which all men have to all things, that is the rights of war will still remain. Next, I distinguish the divers kinds of it, to wit, monarchy, aristocracy, democracy, and paternal dominion, and that of masters over their servants. I declare how they are constituted, and I compare their several conveniences and inconveniences each with other. Furthermore, I unfold what those things are which destroy it, and what his or their duty is who rule in chief. Last of all, I explicate the natures of law, and of sin, and I distinguish law from counsel, from compact, from that which I call right; all which I comprehend under the title of Dominion.

In the last part of it, which is entitled Religion, lest that right which by strong reason I had confirmed the sovereign powers in the preceding discourse have over their subjects, might seem to be repugnant to the sacred Scriptures, I show in the first place how it repugns not the divine right, for as much as God overrules all rulers by nature, that is, by the dictates of natural reason. In the second, for as much as God himself had a peculiar dominion over the Jews by virtue of that ancient covenant of circumcision. In the third, because God doth now rule over us Christians by virtue of our covenant of baptism; and therefore the authority of rulers in chief, or of civil government, is not at all, we see, contrary to religion.

In the last place I declare what duties are necessarily required from us, to enter into the kingdom of heaven; and of those I plainly demonstrate, and conclude out of evident testimonies of holy writ, according to the interpretation made by all, that the obedience which I have affirmed to be due from particular Christian subjects unto their Christian princes cannot possibly in the least sort be repugnant unto Christian religion.

You have seen my method, receive now the reason which moved me to write this. I was studying philosophy for my mind sake, and I had gathered together its first elements in all kinds, and having digested them into three sections by degrees, I thought to have written them so as in the first I would have treated of a body, and its general properties; in the second of man and his special faculties, and affections; in the third, of civil government and the duties of subjects. Wherefore the first section would have contained the first philosophy, and certain elements of physic; in it we would have considered the reasons of time, place, cause, power, relation, proportion, quantity, figure, and motion. In the second we would have been conversant about imagination, memory, intellect, ratiocination, appetite, will, good and evil, honest and dishonest, and the like. What this last section handles, I have now already showed you. Whilst I contrive, order, pensively and slowly compose these matters, (for I only do reason, I dispute not), it so happened in the interim, that my country some few years before the civil wars did rage, was boiling hot with questions concerning the rights of dominion, and the obedience due from subjects, the true forerunners of an approaching war; and was the cause which (all those other matters deferred) ripened, and plucked from me this third part. Therefore it happens that what was last in order, is yet come forth first in time, and the rather, because I saw that grounded on its own principles sufficiently known by experience it would not stand in need of the former sections. I have not yet made it out of a desire of praise (although if I had, I might have defended myself with this fair excuse, that very few do things laudably, who are not affected with commendation) but for your sakes, readers, who I persuaded myself, when you should rightly apprehend and thoroughly understand this doctrine I here present you with, would rather choose to brook with patience some inconveniences under government (because human affairs cannot possibly be without some) than self-opiniatedly disturb the quiet of the public; that, weighing the justice of those things you are about, not by the persuasion and advice of private men, but by the laws of the realm, you will no longer suffer ambitious men through the streams of your blood to wade to their own power; that you will esteem it better to enjoy yourselves in the present state, though perhaps not the best, than by waging war, endeavour to procure a reformation for other men in another age, yourselves in the meanwhile either killed, or consumed with age. Furthermore, for those who will not acknowledge themselves subject to the civil magistrate, and will be exempt from all public burthens, and yet will live under his jurisdiction, and look for protection from the violence and injuries of others, that you would not look on them as fellow-subjects, but esteem them for enemies, and spies, and that ye rashly admit not for God's word all which either openly or privately they shall pretend to be so. I say more plainly, if any preacher, confessor, or casuist, shall but say that this doctrine is agreeable with God's word, namely, that the chief ruler, nay any private man may lawfully be put to death without the chief's command, or that subjects may resist, conspire, or covenant against the supreme power; that ye by no means believe them, but instantly declare their names. He who approves of these reasons, will also like my intentions in writing this book.

Last of all, I have propounded to myself this rule through this whole discourse; first, not to define aught which concerns the justice of single actions, but leave them to be determined by the laws. Next, not to dispute the laws of any government in special, that is, not to point which are the laws of any country, but to declare what the laws of all countries are. Thirdly, not to seem of opinion, that there is a less proportion of obedience due to an aristocracy or democracy, than a monarchy; for though I have endeavoured by arguments in my tenth chapter to gain a belief in men, that monarchy is the most commodious government (which one thing alone I confess in this whole book not to be demonstrated, but only probably stated) yet every where I expressly say, that in all kind of government whatsoever, there ought to be a supreme and equal power. Fourthly, not in anywise to dispute the positions of divines, except those which strip subjects of their obedience, and shake the foundations of civil government. Lastly, lest I might imprudently set forth somewhat of which there would be no need, what I had thus written, I would not presently expose to public interest, wherefore I got some few copies privately dispersed among some of my friends, that discrying the opinions of others, if any things appeared erroneous, hard, or obscure, I might correct, soften, and explain them.

These things I found most bitterly excepted against: that I had made the civil powers too large, but this by ecclesiastical persons; that I had utterly taken away liberty of conscience, but this by sectaries; that I had set princes above the civil laws, but this by lawyers. Wherefore I was not much moved by these men's reprehensions, (as who in doing this did but do their own business) except it were to tie those knots somewhat faster.

But for their sakes who have a little been staggered at the principles themselves, to wit the nature of men, the authority or right of nature, the nature of compacts and contracts, and the original of civil government, because in finding fault they have not so much followed their passions, as their common-sense, I have therefore in some places added some annotations whereby I presumed I might give some satisfaction to their differing thoughts; lastly I have endeavoured to offend none beside those whose principles these contradict, and whose tender minds are lightly offended by every difference of opinions.

Wherefore if ye shall meet with some things which have more of sharpness, and less of certainty than they ought to have, since they are not so much spoken for the maintenance of parties, as the establishment of peace, and by one whose just grief for the present calamities of his country, may very charitably be allowed some liberty, it is his only request to ye, readers, ye will deign to receive them with an equal mind.

Part I: LIBERTY

CHAPTER I

OF THE STATE OF MEN WITHOUT CIVIL SOCIETY

1. THE faculties of human nature may be reduced unto four
kinds; bodily strength, experience, reason, passion. Taking the
beginning of this following doctrine from these, we will declare
in the first place what manner of inclinations men who are endued with these faculties bear towards each other, and whether,
and by what faculty they are born, apt for society, and to preserve themselves against mutual violence; then proceeding, we
will shew what advice was necessary to be taken for this business,
and what are the conditions of society, or of human peace; that
is to say, (changing the words only) what are the fundamental
laws of nature.

2. The greatest part of those men who have written aught
concerning commonwealths, either suppose, or require us, or
beg of us to believe, that man is a creature born fit * for society.

---

* Since we now see actually a constituted society among men, and none
living out of it, since we discern all desirous of congress, and mutual
correspondence, it may seem a wonderful kind of stupidity, to lay in the
very threshold of this doctrine, such a stumbling block before the readers,
as to deny man to be born fit for society. Therefore I must more plainly
say, that it is true indeed, that to man, by nature, or as man, that is, as
soon as he is born, solitude is an enemy; for infants have need of others to
help them to live, and those of riper years to help them to live well, wherefore I deny not that men (even nature compelling) desire to come together.
But civil societies are not mere meetings, but bonds, to the making
whereof, faith and compacts are necessary: the virtue whereof to children,
and fools, and the profit whereof to those who have not yet tasted the
miseries which accompany its defects, is altogether unknown; whence it
happens, that those, because they know not what society is, cannot enter
into it; these, because ignorant of the benefit it brings, care not for it.
Manifest therefore it is, that all men, because they are born in infancy,

The Greeks call him ζῶον πολιτικόν; and on this foundation they so build up the doctrine of civil society, as if for the preservation of peace, and the government of mankind, there were nothing else necessary, than that men should agree to make certain covenants and conditions together, which themselves should then call laws. Which axiom, though received by most, is yet certainly false, and an error proceeding from our too slight contemplation of human nature. For they who shall more narrowly look into the causes for which men come together, and delight in each other's company, shall easily find that this happens not because naturally it could happen no otherwise, but by accident. For if by nature one man should love another (that is) as man, there could no reason be returned why every man should not equally love every man, as being equally man, or why he should rather frequent those whose society affords him honour or profit. We do not therefore by nature seek society for its own sake, but that we may receive some honour or profit from it; these we desire primarily, that secondarily. How, by what advice, men do meet, will be best known by observing those things which they do when they are met. For if they meet for traffic, it is plain every man regards not his fellow, but his business; if to discharge some office, a certain market-friendship is begotten, which hath more of jealousy in it than true love, and whence factions sometimes may arise, but good will never; if for pleasure, and recreation of mind, every man is wont to please himself most with those things which

---

are born unapt for society. Many also (perhaps most men) either through defect of mind, or want of education, remain unfit during the whole course of their lives; yet have they, infants as well as those of riper years, a human nature; wherefore man is made fit for society not by nature, but by education. Furthermore, although man were born in such a condition as to desire it, it follows not, that he therefore were born fit to enter into it; for it is one thing to desire, another to be in capacity fit for what we desire; for even they, who through their pride, will not stoop to equal conditions, without which there can be no society, do yet desire it.

what today we would call, 'socialization'

stir up laughter, whence he may (according to the nature of that which is ridiculous) by comparison of another man's defects and infirmities, pass the more current in his own opinion; and although this be sometimes innocent and without offence, yet it is manifest they are not so much delighted with the society, as their own vain glory. But for the most part, in these kinds of meetings, we wound the absent; their whole life, sayings, actions are examined, judged, condemned; nay, it is very rare, but some present receive a fling before they part, so as his reason was not ill, who was wont always at parting to go out last. And these are indeed the true delights of society, unto which we are carried by nature, that is, by those passions which are incident to all creatures, until either by sad experience, or good precepts, it so fall out (which in many never happens) that the appetite of present matters be dulled with the memory of things past, without which, the discourse of most quick and nimble men on this subject, is but cold and hungry.

But if it so happen, that being met, they pass their time in relating some stories, and one of them begins to tell one which concerns himself; instantly every one of the rest most greedily desires to speak of himself too; if one relate some wonder, the rest will tell you miracles, if they have them, if not, they will feign them. Lastly, that I may say somewhat of them who pretend to be wiser than others; if they meet to talk of philosophy, look how many men, so many would be esteemed masters, or else they not only love not their fellows, but even persecute them with hatred. So clear is it by experience to all men who a little more narrowly consider human affairs, that all free congress ariseth either from mutual poverty, or from vain glory, whence the parties met, endeavour to carry with them either some benefit, or to leave behind them that same εὐδοκιμεῖν some esteem and honour with those, with whom they have been conversant. The same is also collected by reason out of the defini-

tions themselves, of will, good, honour, profitable. For when
we voluntarily contract society, in all manner of society we look
after the object of the will, that is, that, which every one of
those who gather together, propounds to himself for good. Now
whatsoever seems good, is pleasant, and relates either to the
senses, or the mind. But all the mind's pleasure is either glory,
(or to have a good opinion of one's self) or refers to glory in
the end; the rest are sensual, or conducing to sensuality, which
may be all comprehended under the word conveniences. All
society therefore is either for gain, or for glory; that is, not so
much for love of our fellows, as for the love of ourselves. But
no society can be great, or lasting, which begins from vain
glory; because that glory is like honour, if all men have it, no
man hath it, for they consist in comparison and precellence;
neither doth the society of others advance any whit the cause
of my glorying in myself; for every man must account himself,
such as he can make himself, without the help of others. But
though the benefits of this life may be much farthered by mutual
help, since yet those may be better attained to by dominion,
than by the society of others: I hope no body will doubt but
that men would much more greedily be carried by nature, if
all fear were removed, to obtain dominion, than to gain society.
We must therefore resolve, that the original of all great and
lasting societies consisted not in the mutual good will men had
towards each other, but in the mutual fear * they had of each
other.

*It is objected: it is so improbable that men should grow into civil
societies out of fear, that if they had been afraid, they would not have
endured each other's looks. They presume, I believe, that to fear is nothing
else than to be affrighted. I comprehend in this word fear, a certain fore-
sight of future evil; neither do I conceive flight the sole property of fear,
but to distrust, suspect, take heed, provide so that they may not fear, is
also incident to the fearful. They who go to sleep, shut their doors; they
who travel, carry their swords with them, because they fear thieves.
Kingdoms guard their coasts and frontiers with forts and castles; cities

3. The cause of mutual fear consists partly in the natural
equality of men, partly in their mutual will of hurting: whence
it comes to pass that we can neither expect from others, nor
promise to ourselves the least security. For if we look on men
full-grown, and consider how brittle the frame of our human
body is, (which perishing, all its strength, vigour, and wisdom
itself perisheth with it) and how easy a matter it is, even for
the weakest man to kill the strongest, there is no reason why
any man trusting to his own strength should conceive himself
made by nature above others: they are equals who can do
equal things one against the other; but they who can do the
greatest things, (namely, kill) can do equal things. All men
therefore among themselves are by nature equal; the inequality
we now discern, hath its spring from the civil law.

4. All men in the state of nature have a desire and will to
hurt, but not proceeding from the same cause, neither equally
to be condemned. For one man, according to that natural
equality which is among us, permits as much to others, as he
assumes to himself (which is an argument of a temperate
man, and one that rightly values his power). Another, supposing himself above others, will have a license to do what he lists,
and challenges respect and honour, as due to him before others,
(which is an argument of a fiery spirit). This man's will to
hurt ariseth from vain glory, and the false esteem he hath of
his own strength; the other's, from the necessity of defending

---

are compact with walls, and all for fear of neighbouring kingdoms and
towns; even the strongest armies, and most accomplished for fight, yet
sometimes parley for peace, as fearing each other's power, and lest they
might be overcome. It is through fear that men secure themselves, by
flight indeed, and in corners, if they think they cannot escape otherwise;
but for the most part by arms and defensive weapons; whence it happens,
that daring to come forth, they know each other's spirits; but then, if
they fight, civil society ariseth from the victory, if they agree, from their
agreement.

himself, his liberty, and his goods, against this man's violence.

5. Furthermore, since the combat of wits is the fiercest, the greatest discords which are, must necessarily arise from this contention. For in this case it is not only odious to contend against, but also not to consent. For not to approve of what a man saith, is no less than tacitly to accuse him of an error in that thing which he speaketh; as in very many things to dissent, is as much as if you accounted him a fool whom you dissent from; which may appear hence, that there are no wars so sharply waged as between sects of the same religion, and factions of the same commonweal, where the contestation is either concerning doctrines or politic prudence. And since all the pleasure and jollity of the mind consists in this, even to get some, with whom comparing, it may find somewhat wherein to triumph and vaunt itself; it is impossible but men must declare sometimes some mutual scorn and contempt, either by laughter, or by words, or by gesture, or some sign or other; than which there is no greater vexation of mind, and than from which there cannot possibly arise a greater desire to do hurt.

6. But the most frequent reason why men desire to hurt each other, ariseth hence, that many men at the same time have an appetite to the same thing; which yet very often they can neither enjoy in common, nor yet divide it; whence it follows that the strongest must have it, and who is strongest must be decided by the sword.

7. Among so many dangers therefore, as the natural lusts of men do daily threaten each other withal, to have a care of one's self is not a matter so scornfully to be looked upon, as if so be there had not been a power and will left in one to have done otherwise. For every man is desirous of what is good for him, and shuns what is evil, but chiefly the chiefest of natural evils, which is death; and this he doth, by a certain impulsion of nature, no less than that whereby a stone moves downward.

It is therefore neither absurd, nor reprehensible, neither against
the dictates of true reason, for a man to use all his endeavours
to preserve and defend his body and the members thereof from
death and sorrows. But that which is not contrary to right
reason, that all men account to be done justly, and with right;
neither by the word right is anything else signified, than that
liberty which every man hath to make use of his natural faculties according to right reason. Therefore the first foundation of
natural right is this, that every man as much as in him lies endeavour to protect his life and members.

8. But because it is in vain for a man to have a right to the
end, if the right to the necessary means be denied him; it follows, that since every man hath a right to preserve himself, he
must also be allowed a right to use all the means, and do all
the actions, without which he cannot preserve himself.

9. Now whether the means which he is about to use, and
the action he is performing, be necessary to the preservation
of his life and members, or not, he himself, by the right of
nature, must be judge. For say another man judge that it is
contrary to right reason that I should judge of mine own peril:
why now, because he judgeth of what concerns me, by the
same reason, because we are equal by nature, will I judge also
of things which do belong to him. Therefore it agrees with
right reason, that is, it is the right of nature that I judge of his
opinion, that is, whether it conduce to my preservation, or not.

10. Nature hath given to every one a right to all; that is, it
was lawful for every man in the bare state of nature,* or before

---

* This is thus to be understood: what any man does in the bare state
of nature is injurious to no man; not that in such a state he cannot offend
God, or break the laws of nature; for injustice against men presupposeth
human laws, such as in the state of nature there are none. Now the
truth of this proposition thus conceived is sufficiently demonstrated to
the mindful reader in the articles immediately foregoing; but because in
certain cases the difficulty of the conclusion makes us forget the premises,

such time as men had engaged themselves by any covenants or bonds, to do what he would, and against whom he thought fit, and to possess, use, and enjoy all what he would, or could get. Now because whatsoever a man would, it therefore seems good to him because he wills is, and either it really doth, or at least seems to him to contribute towards his preservation, (but we have already allowed him to be judge, in the foregoing article, whether it doth or not, in so much as we are to hold all for necessary whatsoever he shall esteem so), and by the 7th article it appears that by the right of nature those things may be done, and must be had, which necessarily conduce to the protection of life and members, it follows, that in the state of nature, to have all, and do all, is lawful for all. And this is that which is meant by that common saying, nature hath given all to all, from whence we understand likewise, that in the state of nature, profit is the measure of right.

11. But it was the least benefit for men thus to have a common right to all things; for the effects of this right are the same, almost, as if there had been no right at all. For although any man might say of every thing, this is mine, yet could he not

---

I will contract this argument, and make it most evident to a single view. Every man hath right to protect himself, as appears by the seventh article. The same man therefore hath a right to use all the means which necessarily conduce to this end, by the eighth article. But those are the necessary means which he shall judge to be such, by the ninth article. He therefore hath a right to make use of, and to do all whatsoever he shall judge requisite for his preservation: wherefore by the judgment of him that doth it, the thing done is either right, or wrong, and therefore right. True it is therefore in the bare state of nature, &c. But if any man pretend somewhat to tend necessarily to his preservation, which yet he himself doth not confidently believe so, he may offend against the laws of nature, as in the third chapter of this book is more at large declared. It hath been objected by some: if a son kill his father, doth he him no injury? I have answered, that a son cannot be understood to be at any time in the state of nature, as being under the power and command of them to whom he owes his protection as soon as ever he is born, namely, either his father's or his mother's, or his that nourished him, as is demonstrated in the ninth chapter.

right – determined via profit

right – determined via rewards

But if All have All
none have none

enjoy it, by reason of his neighbour, who having equal right, and equal power, would pretend the same thing to be his.

12. If now to this natural proclivity of men, to hurt each other, which they derive from their passions, but chiefly from a vain esteem of themselves, you add, the right of all to all, wherewith one by right invades, the other by right resists, and whence arise perpetual jealousies and suspicions on all hands, and how hard a thing it is to provide against an enemy invading us, with an intention to oppress, and ruin, though he come with a small number, and no great provision; it cannot be denied but that the natural state of men, before they entered into society, was a mere war, and that not simply, but a war of all men against all men. For what is war, but that same time in which the will of contesting by force is fully declared, either by words, or deeds? The time remaining, is termed peace.

13. But it is easily judged how disagreeable a thing to the preservation either of mankind, or of each single man, a perpetual war is. But it is perpetual in its own nature, because in regard of the equality of those that strive, it cannot be ended by victory; for in this state the conqueror is subject to so much danger, as it were to be accounted a miracle, if any, even the most strong, should close up his life with many years, and old age. They of America are examples hereof, even in this present age: other nations have been in former ages, which now indeed are become civil and flourishing, but were then few, fierce, short-lived, poor, nasty, and deprived of all that pleasure, and beauty of life, which peace and society are wont to bring with them. Whosoever therefore holds, that it had been best to have continued in that state in which all things were lawful for all men, he contradicts himself. For every man by natural necessity desires that which is good for him: nor is there any that esteems a war of all against all, which necessarily adheres to such a state, to be good for him. And so it happens, that through fear of each other we think it fit to rid ourselves of this con-

dition, and to get some fellows; that if there needs must be war, it may not yet be against all men, nor without some helps.

14. Fellows are gotten either by constraint, or by consent; by constraint, when after fight the conqueror makes the conquered serve him either through fear of death, or by laying fetters on him: by consent, when men enter into society to help each other, both parties consenting without any constraint. But the conqueror may by right compel the conquered, or the strongest the weaker, (as a man in health may one that is sick, or he that is of riper years a child) unless he will choose to die, to give caution of his future obedience. For since the right of protecting ourselves according to our own wills proceeded from our danger, and our danger from our equality, it is more consonant to reason, and more certain for our conservation, using the present advantage to secure ourselves by taking caution, than, when they shall be full grown and strong, and got out of our power, to endeavour to recover that power again by doubtful fight. And on the other side, nothing can be thought more absurd, than by discharging whom you already have weak in your power, to make him at once both an enemy, and a strong one. From whence we may understand likewise as a corollary in the natural state of men, that a sure and irresistible power confers the right of dominion and ruling over those who cannot resist; insomuch, as the right of all things, that can be done, adheres essentially and immediately unto this omnipotence hence arising.

15. Yet cannot men expect any lasting preservation continuing thus in the state of nature, that is, of war, by reason of that equality of power, and other human faculties they are endued withal. Wherefore to seek peace, where there is any hopes of obtaining it, and where there is none, to enquire out for auxiliaries of war, is the dictate of right reason, that is, the law of nature, as shall be showed in the next chapter.

Chapter II

Of the Law of Nature Concerning Contracts

1. ALL authors agree not concerning the definition of the natural law, who notwithstanding do very often make use of this term in their writings. The method therefore, wherein we begin from definitions and exclusion of all equivocation, is only proper to them who leave no place for contrary disputes. For the rest, if any man say, that somewhat is done against the law of nature, one proves it hence, because it was done against the general agreement of all the most wise and learned nations: but this declares not who shall be the judge of the wisdom and learning of all nations. Another hence, that it was done against the general consent of all mankind; which definition is by no means to be admitted. For then it were impossible for any but children and fools, to offend against such a law; for sure, under the notion of mankind, they comprehend all men actually endued with reason. These therefore either do nought against it, or if they do aught, it is without their joint accord, and therefore ought to be excused. But to receive the laws of nature from the consents of them, who oftener break, than observe them, is in truth unreasonable. Besides, men condemn the same things in others, which they approve in themselves; on the other side, they publicly commend what they privately condemn; and they deliver their opinions more by hearsay, than any speculation of their own; and they accord more through hatred of some object, through fear, hope, love, or some other perturbation of mind, than true reason. And therefore it comes to pass, that whole bodies of people often do those things by

31

general accord, or contention, which those writers most willingly acknowledge to be against the law of nature. But since
all do grant that is done by right, which is not done against
reason, we ought to judge those actions only wrong, which are
repugnant to right reason, that is, which contradict some certain truth collected by right reasoning from true principles.
But that wrong which is done, we say it is done against some
law. Therefore true reason is a certain law, which (since it is
no less a part of human nature, than any other faculty, or
affection of the mind) is also termed natural. Therefore the
law of nature, that I may define it, is the dictate of right
reason,* conversant about those things which are either to
be done or omitted for the constant preservation of life and
members, as much as in us lies.

2. But the first and fundamental law of nature is, that peace
is to be sought after, where it may be found; and where not,
there to provide ourselves for helps of war. For we showed in
the last article of the foregoing chapter, that this precept is
the dictate of right reason; but that the dictates of right reason

---

* By right reason in the natural state of men, I understand not, as
many do, an infallible faculty, but the act of reasoning, that is, the
peculiar and true ratiocination of every man concerning those actions
of his which may either redound to the damage or benefit of his neighbours. I call it peculiar, because although in a civil government the
reason of the supreme, that is, the civil law, is to be received by each
single subject for the right; yet being without this civil government, (in
which state no man can know right reason from false, but by comparing
it with his own) every man's own reason is to be accounted, not only
the rule of his own actions which are done at his own peril, but also
for the measure of another man's reason, in such things as do concern
him. I call it true, that is, concluding from true principles rightly framed,
because that the whole breach of the laws of nature consists in the false
reasoning, or rather folly of those men who see not those duties they are
necessarily to perform towards others in order to their own conservation.
But the principles of right reasoning about such like duties are those
which are explained in the second, third, fourth, fifth, sixth, and seventh
articles of the first chapter.

are natural laws, that hath been newly proved above. But this is the first, because the rest are derived from this, and they direct the ways either to peace or self-defence.

3. But one of the natural laws derived from this fundamental one is this: that the right of all men to all things, ought not to be retained, but that some certain rights ought to be transferred, or relinquished. For if every one should retain his right to all things, it must necessarily follow, that some by right might invade, and others, by the same right, might defend themselves against them, (for every man, by natural necessity, endeavours to defend his body, and the things which he judgeth necessary towards the protection of his body). Therefore war would follow. He therefore acts against the reason of peace, that is, against the law of nature, whosoever he be, that doth not part with his right to all things.

4. But he is said to part with his right, who either absolutely renounceth it, or conveys it to another. He absolutely renounceth it, who by some sufficient sign, or meet tokens, declares that he is willing that it shall never be lawful for him to do that again, which before, by right, he might have done. But he conveys it to another, who by some sufficient sign, or meet tokens, declares to that other, that he is willing it should be unlawful for him to resist him, in going about to do somewhat in the performance whereof he might before, with right, have resisted him. But that the conveyance of right consists merely in not resisting, is understood by this, that before it was conveyed, he, to whom he conveyed it, had even then also a right to all, whence he could not give any new right: but the resisting right he had, before he gave it, by reason whereof the other could not freely enjoy his rights, is utterly abolished. Whosoever therefore acquires some right in the natural state of men, he only procures himself security, and freedom from just molestation in the enjoyment of his primitive right: as for

example, if any man shall sell or give away a farm, he utterly deprives himself only from all right to this farm, but he does not so from others also.

5. But in the conveyance of right, the will is requisite not only of him that conveys, but of him also that accepts it. If either be wanting, the right remains: for if I would have given what was mine to one who refused to accept of it, I have not therefore either simply renounced my right, or conveyed it to any man. For the cause which moved me to part with it to this man, was in him only, not in others too.

6. But if there be no other token extant of our will either to quit, or convey our right, but only words; those words must either relate to the present, or time past; for if they be of the future only, they convey nothing. For example, he that speaks thus of the time to come, I will give to-morrow, declares openly that yet he hath not given it: so that all this day his right remains, and abides to-morrow too, unless in the interim he actually bestows it: for what is mine, remains mine till I have parted with it. But if I shall speak of the time present, suppose thus; I do give or have given you this to be received to-morrow, by these words is signified that I have already given it, and that his right to receive it to-morrow, is conveyed to him by me to-day.

7. Nevertheless, although words alone are not sufficient tokens to declare the will; if yet to words relating to the future, there shall some other signs be added, they may become as valid, as if they had been spoken of the present. If therefore, as by reason of those other signs, it appear that he that speaks of the future, intends those words should be effectual toward the perfect transferring of his right, they ought to be valid; for the conveyance of right depends not on words, but (as hath been instanced in the fourth article) on the declaration of the will.

8. If any man convey some part of his right to another, and doth not this for some certain benefit received, or for some compact, a conveyance in this kind is called a gift, or free donation. But in free donation those words only oblige us which signify the present, or the time past; for if they respect the future, they oblige not as words, for the reason given in the foregoing article. It must needs therefore be, that the obligation arise from some other tokens of the will. But, because whatsoever is voluntarily done, is done for some good to him that wills it; there can no other token be assigned of the will to give it, except some benefit either already received, or to be acquired. But it is supposed that no such benefit is acquired, nor any compact in being; for if so, it would cease to be a free gift. It remains therefore, that a mutual good turn without agreement be expected; but no sign can be given, that he, who used future words toward him who was in no sort engaged to return a benefit, should desire to have his words so understood, as to oblige himself thereby. Nor is it suitable to reason, that those who are easily inclined to do well to others, should be obliged by every promise, testifying their present good affection. And for this cause, a promiser in this kind must be understood to have time to deliberate, and power to change that affection, as well as he to whom he made that promise, may alter his desert. But he that deliberates, is so far forth free, nor can be said to have already given. But if he promise often, and yet give seldom, he ought to be condemned of levity, and be called not a donor, but doson.

9. But the act of two, or more, mutually conveying their rights, is called a contract. But in every contract, either both parties instantly perform what they contract for, insomuch as there is no trust had from either to other; or the one performs, the other is trusted; or neither perform. Where both parties perform presently, there the contract is ended, as soon as it is

performed; but where there is credit given either to one or both, there the party trusted promiseth after-performance; and this kind of promise is called a covenant.

10. But the covenant made by the party trusted with him who hath already performed, although the promise be made by words pointing at the future, doth no less transfer the right of future time, than if it had been made by words signifying the present or time past. For the other's performance is a most manifest sign that he so understood the speech of him whom he trusted, as that he would certainly make performance also at the appointed time; and by this sign the party trusted knew himself to be thus understood, which, because he hindered not, was an evident token of his will to perform. The promises therefore which are made for some benefit received (which are also covenants) are tokens of the will; that is, (as in the foregoing section hath been declared) of the last act of deliberating, whereby the liberty of non-performance is abolished, and by consequence are obligatory. For where liberty ceaseth, there beginneth obligation.

11. But the covenants which are made in contract of mutual trust, neither party performing out of hand, if there arise * a just suspicion in either of them, are in the state of nature invalid. For he that first performs, by reason of the wicked disposition of the greatest part of men studying their own advantage, either by right or wrong, exposeth himself to the perverse will of him with whom he hath contracted. For it suits not with reason, that any man should perform first, if it be not likely that the other will make good his promise after; which, whether it be probable or not, he that doubts it,

---

* For, except there appear some new cause of fear, either from somewhat done, or some other token of the will not to perform from the other part, it cannot be judged to be a just fear; for the cause which was not sufficient to keep him from making compact, must not suffice to authorize the breach of it, being made.

must be judge of, as hath been showed in the foregoing chapter in the ninth article. Thus, I say, things stand in the state
of nature. But in a civil state, when there is a power which
can compel both parties, he that hath contracted to perform
first, must first perform; because, that since the other may be
compelled, the cause which made him fear the other's non-
performance, ceaseth.

12. But from this reason, that in all free gifts and compacts,
there is an acceptance of the conveyance of right required: it
follows, that no man can compact with him who doth not
declare his acceptance. And therefore we cannot compact with
beasts, neither can we give or take from them any manner
of right, by reason of their want of speech and understanding.
Neither can any man covenant with God, or be obliged to him
by vow, except so far forth as it appears to him by Holy Scriptures, that he hath substituted certain men who have authority
to accept of such-like vows and covenants, as being in God's
stead.

13. Those therefore do vow in vain, who are in the state of
nature, where they are not tied by any civil law, (except by
most certain revelation the will of God to accept their vow
or pact, be made known to them). For if what they vow be
contrary to the law of nature, they are not tied by their vow,
for no man is tied to perform an unlawful act. But if what is
vowed, be commanded by some law of nature, it is not their
vow, but the law itself which ties them. But if he were free
before his vow, either to do it or not do it, his liberty remains,
because that the openly declared will of the obliger is requisite
to make an obligation by vow, which in the case propounded
is supposed not to be. Now I call him the obliger, to whom
any one is tied, and the obliged, him who is tied.

14. Covenants are made of such things only as fall under
our deliberation, for it can be no covenant without the will of

the contractor, but the will is the last act of him who deliberates; wherefore they only concern things possible and to
come. No man, therefore, by his compact, obligeth himself to
an impossibility. But yet, though we often covenant to do such
things as then seemed possible when we promised them, which
yet afterward appear to be impossible, are we therefore freed
from all obligation? The reason whereof is, that he who promiseth a future, in certainty receives a present benefit, on condition that he return another for it. For his will, who performs
the present benefit, hath simply before it, for its object, a certain good valuable with the thing promised; but the thing itself
not simply, but with condition if it could be done. But if it
should so happen, that even this should prove impossible, why
then he must perform as much as he can. Covenants, therefore,
oblige us not to perform just the thing itself covenanted for,
but our utmost endeavour; for this only is, the things themselves are not in our power.

15. We are freed from covenants two ways, either by performing, or by being forgiven. By performing, for beyond that
we obliged not ourselves. By being forgiven, because he whom
we obliged ourselves to, by forgiving, is conceived to return
us that right which we passed over to him. For forgiving implies giving, that is, by the fourth article of this chapter, a
conveyance of right to him to whom the gift is made.

16. It is a usual question, whether compacts extorted from
us through fear, do oblige, or not: for example, if, to redeem
my life from the power of a robber, I promise to pay him
100l. next day, and that I will do no act whereby to apprehend and bring him to justice, whether I am tied to keep
promise or not. But though such a promise must sometimes be
judged to be of no effect, yet it is not to be accounted so because it proceedeth from fear. For then it would follow, that
those promises which reduced men to a civil life, and by which

laws were made, might likewise be of none effect; (for it proceeds from fear of mutual slaughter, that one man submits
himself to the dominion of another); and he should play the
fool finely, who should trust his captive covenanting with the
price of his redemption. It holds universally true, that promises
do oblige when there is some benefit received, and when to
promise, and the thing promised, be lawful. But it is lawful,
for the redemption of my life, both to promise, and to give what
I will of mine own to any man, even to a thief. We are obliged,
therefore, by promises proceeding from fear, except the civil law
forbid them, by virtue whereof, that which is promised becomes
unlawful.

17. Whosoever shall contract with one to do or omit somewhat, and shall after covenant the contrary with another, he
maketh not the former, but the latter contract unlawful. For
he hath no longer right to do, or to omit aught, who by former
contracts hath conveyed it to another. Wherefore he can convey no right by latter contracts, and what is promised, is
promised without right. He is therefore tied only to his first
contract; to break which is unlawful.

18. No man is obliged by any contracts whatsoever not to
resist him who shall offer to kill, wound, or any other way
hurt his body. For there is in every man a certain high degree
of fear, through which he apprehends that evil which is done
to him to be the greatest; and therefore by natural necessity
he shuns it all he can, and it is supposed he can do no otherwise. When a man is arrived to this degree of fear, we cannot
expect but he will provide for himself either by flight or fight.
Since therefore no man is tied to impossibilities, they who are
threatened either with death, (which is the greatest evil to
nature) or wounds, or some other bodily hurts, and are not
stout enough to bear them, are not obliged to endure them.
Furthermore, he that is tied by contract is trusted, (for faith

only is the bond of contracts) but they who are brought to punishment, either capital, or more gentle, are fettered, or strongly guarded, which is a most certain sign that they seemed not sufficiently bound from non-resistance by their contracts. It is one thing, if I promise thus: if I do it not at the day appointed, kill me. Another thing, if thus: if I do it not, though you should offer to kill me, I will not resist. All men, if need be, contract the first way, but there is need sometimes. This second way, none; neither is it ever needful; for in the mere state of nature, if you have a mind to kill, that state itself affords you a right; insomuch as you need not first trust him, if for breach of trust you will afterwards kill him. But in a civil state, where the right of life, and death, and of all corporal punishment is with the supreme; that same right of killing cannot be granted to any private person. Neither need the supreme himself contract with any man patiently to yield to his punishment, but only this, that no man offer to defend others from him. If in the state of nature, as between two realms, there should a contract be made, on condition of killing if it were not performed, we must presuppose another contract of not killing before the appointed day. Wherefore on that day, if there be no performance, the right of war returns, that is an hostile state, in which all things are lawful, and therefore resistance also. Lastly, by the contract of not resisting, we are obliged of two evils to make choice of that which seems the greater; for certain death is a greater evil than fighting. But of two evils it is impossible not to choose the least. By such a compact, therefore, we should be tied to impossibilities, which is contrary to the very nature of compacts.

19. Likewise no man is tied by any compacts whatsoever to accuse himself, or any other, by whose damage he is like to procure himself a bitter life. Wherefore neither is a father obliged to bear witness against his son, nor a husband against

his wife, nor a son against his father, nor any man against any one by whose means he hath his subsistence; for in vain is that testimony which is presumed to be corrupted from nature. But although no man be tied to accuse himself by any compact, yet in a public trial he may, by torture, be forced to make answer. But such answers are no testimony of the fact, but helps for the searching out of truth; insomuch that whether the party tortured answer true or false, or whether he answer not at all, whatsoever he doth, he doth it by right.

20. Swearing is a speech joined to a promise, whereby the promiser declares his renouncing of God's mercy, unless he perform his word. Which definition is contained in the words themselves, which have in them the very essence of an oath, to wit, so God help me, or other equivalent, as with the Romans, do thou Jupiter so destroy the deceiver, as I slay this same beast. Neither is this any let, but that an oath may as well sometimes be affirmatory as promissory; for he that confirms his affirmation with an oath, promiseth that he speaks truth. But though in some places it was the fashion for subjects to swear by their kings, that custom took its original hence, that those kings took upon them divine honour. For oaths were therefore introduced, that by religion, and consideration of the divine power, men might have a greater dread of breaking their faiths, than that wherewith they fear men, from whose eyes their actions may lie hid.

21. Whence it follows, that an oath must be conceived in that form, which he useth, who takes it; for in vain is any man brought to swear by a God whom he believes not, and therefore neither fears him. For though by the light of nature it may be known that there is a God, yet no man thinks he is to swear by him in any other fashion, or by any other name, than what is contained in the precepts of his own proper, that is (as he who swears imagines) the true religion.

22. By the definition of an oath we may understand, that a bare contract obligeth no less, than that to which we are sworn. For it is the contract which binds us; the oath relates to the divine punishment, which it could not provoke, if the breach of contract were not in itself unlawful; but it could not be unlawful, if the contract were not obligatory. Furthermore, he that renounceth the mercy of God, obligeth himself not to any punishment; because it is ever lawful to deprecate the punishment, howsoever provoked, and to enjoy God's pardon if it be granted. The only effect therefore of an oath is this, to cause men who are naturally inclined to break all manner of faith, through fear of punishment, to make the more conscience of their words and actions.

23. To exact an oath, where the breach of contract, if any be made, cannot but be known, and where the party compacted withal wants not power to punish, is to do somewhat more than is necessary unto self-defence, and shews a mind desirous not so much to benefit itself, as to prejudice another. For an oath, out of the very form of swearing, is taken in order to the provocation of God's anger, that is to say, of him that is omnipotent, against those who therefore violate their faith, because they think that by their own strength they can escape the punishment of men; and of him that is omniscient, against those who therefore usually break their trust, because they hope that no man shall see them.

CHAPTER III

OF THE OTHER LAWS OF NATURE

1. ANOTHER of the laws of nature is, to perform contracts, or to keep trust; for it hath been showed in the foregoing chapter, that the law of nature commands every man, as a thing necessary, to obtain peace, to convey certain rights from each to other; and that this (as often as it shall happen to be done) is called a contract. But this is so far forth only conducible to peace, as we shall perform ourselves what we contract with others shall be done or omitted; and in vain would contracts be made, unless we stood to them. Because therefore, to stand to our covenants, or to keep faith, is a thing necessary for the obtaining of peace, it will prove, by the second article of the second chapter, to be a precept of the natural law.

2. Neither is there in this matter any exception of the persons with whom we contract, as if they keep no faith with others, or hold that none ought to be kept, or are guilty of any other kind of vice. For he that contracts, in that he doth contract, denies that action to be in vain; and it is against reason for a knowing man to do a thing in vain; and if he think himself not bound to keep it, in thinking so he affirms the contract to be made in vain. He therefore who contracts with one with whom he thinks he is not bound to keep faith, he doth at once think a contract to be a thing done in vain, and not in vain; which is absurd. Either therefore we must hold trust with all men, or else not bargain with them; that is, either there must be a declared war, or a sure and faithful peace.

3. The breaking of a bargain, as also the taking back of a

gift, (which ever consists in some action or omission) is called
an injury. But that action or omission is called unjust, insomuch as an injury, and an unjust action or omission, signify
the same thing, and both are the same with breach of contract and trust. And it seems the word injury came to be given
to any action or omission, because they were without right;
he that acted or omitted, having before conveyed his right to
some other. And there is some likeness between that which in
the common course of life we call injury, and that which in the
Schools is usually called absurd. For even as he who by arguments is driven to deny the assertion which he first maintained, is said to be brought to an absurdity; in like manner,
he who through weakness of mind does or omits that which
before he had by contract promised not to do or omit, commits
an injury, and falls into no less contradiction than he who in the
Schools is reduced to an absurdity. For by contracting for some
future action, he wills it done; by not doing it, he wills it not
done: which is to will a thing done and not done at the same
time, which is a contradiction. An injury therefore is a kind
of absurdity in conversation, as an absurdity is a kind of injury
in disputation.

4. From these grounds it follows, that an injury can be done
to no man * but him with whom we enter covenant, or to

* The word injustice relates to some law: injury, to some person, as
well as some law. For what is unjust, is unjust to all; but there may an
injury be done, and yet not against me, nor thee, but some other; and
sometimes against no private person, but the magistrate only; sometimes
also neither against the magistrate, nor any private man, but only against
God. For through contract and conveyance of right, we say, that an injury is done against this or that man. Hence it is (which we see in all
kind of government) that what private men contract between themselves
by word or writing, is released again at the will of the obliger. But those
mischiefs which are done against the laws of the land, as theft, homicide,
and the like, are punished, not as he wills, to whom the hurt is done,
but according to the will of the magistrate; that is, the constituted laws.

whom somewhat is made over by deed of gift, or to whom somewhat is promised by way of bargain. And therefore damaging and injuring are often disjoined. For if a master command his servant, who hath promised to obey him, to pay a sum of money, or carry some present to a third man; the servant, if he do it not, hath indeed damaged this third party, but he injured his master only. So also in a civil government, if any man offend another with whom he hath made no contract, he damages him to whom the evil is done, but he injures none but him to whom the power of government belongs. For if he who receives the hurt should expostulate the mischief, he that did it should answer thus: what art thou to me; why should I rather do according to yours than mine own will, since I do not hinder, but you may do your own, and not my mind? In which speech, where there hath no manner of precontract passed, I see not, I confess, what is reprehensible.

5. These words, just and unjust, as also justice and injustice, are equivocal; for they signify one thing when they are attributed to persons, another when to actions. When they are attributed to actions, just signifies as much as what is done with right, and unjust, as what is done with injury. He who hath done some just thing, is not therefore said to be a just person, but guiltless; and he that hath done some unjust thing, we do not therefore say he is an unjust, but guilty man. But when the words are applied to persons, to be just signifies as much as to be delighted in just dealing, to study how to do righteousness, or to endeavour in all things to do that which is just; and to be unjust is to neglect righteous dealing, or to think it is to be measured not according to my contract, but some present benefit. So as the justice or injustice of the mind, the intention, or the man, is one thing, that of an action, or omission, another; and innumerable actions of a just man may be unjust, and of an unjust man, just. But that man is to be ac-

counted just, who doth just things because the law commands it, unjust things only by reason of his infirmity; and he is properly said to be unjust, who doth righteousness for fear of the punishment annexed unto the law, and unrighteousness by reason of the iniquity of his mind.

6. The justice of actions is commonly distinguished into two kinds, commutative and distributive; the former whereof, they say, consists in arithmetical, the latter in geometrical proportion, and that is conversant in exchanging, in buying, selling, borrowing, lending, location and conduction, and other acts whatsoever belonging to contractors, where, if there be an equal return made, hence, they say, springs a commutative justice: but this is busied about the dignity and merits of men, so as if there be rendered to every man κατὰ τὴν ἀξίαν, more to him who is more worthy, and less to him that deserves less, and that proportionably, hence, they say, ariseth distributive justice. I acknowledge here some certain distinction of equality: to wit, that one is an equality simply so called, as when two things of equal value are compared together, as a pound of silver with twelve ounces of the same silver; the other is an equality *secundum quod,* as when a thousand pounds is to be divided to a hundred men, six hundred pounds are given to sixty men, and four hundred to forty, where there is no equality between six hundred and four hundred; but when it happens that there is the same inequality in the number of them to whom it is distributed, every one of them shall take an equal part, whence it is called an equal distribution. But such like equality is the same thing with geometrical proportion. But what is all this to justice? For neither if I sell my goods for as much as I can get for them, do I injure the buyer, who sought and desired them of me; neither if I divide more of what is mine to him who deserves less, so long as I give the other what I have agreed for, do I wrong to either. Which truth our

Saviour himself, being God, testifies in the Gospel. This therefore is no distinction of justice, but of equality. Yet perhaps it
cannot be denied but that justice is a certain equality, as consisting in this only; that since we are all equal by nature, one
should not arrogate more right to himself, than he grants to
another, unless he have fairly gotten it by compact. And let
this suffice to be spoken against this distinction of justice, although now almost generally received by all, lest any man
should conceive an injury to be somewhat else than the breach
of faith or contract, as hath been defined above.

7. It is an old saying, *volenti non fit injuria,* the willing
man receives no injury; yet the truth of it may be derived from
our principles. For grant that a man be willing that that should
be done which he conceives to be an injury to him; why then,
that is done by his will, which by contract was not lawful to
be done. But he being willing that should be done which was
not lawful by contract, the contract itself (by the fifteenth
article of the foregoing chapter) becomes void. The right therefore of doing it returns; therefore it is done by right; wherefore
it is no injury.

8. The third precept of the natural law is, that you suffer
not him to be the worse for you, who, out of the confidence he
had in you, first did you a good turn; or that you accept not
a gift, but with a mind to endeavour, that the giver shall have
no just occasion to repent him of his gift. For without this, he
should act without reason, that would confer a benefit where
he sees it would be lost; and by this means all beneficence, and
trust, together with all kind of benevolence, would be taken
from among men, neither would there be aught of mutual
assistance among them, nor any commencement of gaining
grace and favour; by reason whereof the state of war would
necessarily remain, contrary to the fundamental law of nature.
But because the breach of this law is not a breach of trust or

contract, (for we suppose no contracts to have passed among them), therefore is it not usually termed an injury; but because good turns and thanks have a mutual eye to each other, it is called ingratitude.

9. The fourth precept of nature is, that every man render himself useful unto others: which, that we may rightly understand, we must remember that there is in men a diversity of dispositions to enter into society, arising from the diversity of their affections, not unlike that which is found in stones, brought together in the building, by reason of the diversity of their matter and figure. For as a stone, which in regard of its sharp and angular form takes up more room from other stones than it fills up itself, neither because of the hardness of its matter can not well be pressed together, or easily cut, and would hinder the building from being fitly compacted, is cast away, as not fit for use: so a man, for the harshness of his disposition in retaining superfluities for himself, and detaining of necessaries from others, and being incorrigible by reason of the stubbornness of his affections, is commonly said to be useless and troublesome unto others. Now, because each one not by right only, but even by natural necessity, is supposed with all his main might to intend the procurement of those things which are necessary to his own preservation; if any man will contend on the other side for superfluities, by his default there will arise a war; because that on him alone there lay no necessity of contending; he therefore acts against the fundamental law of nature. Whence it follows, (which we were to show), that it is a precept of nature, that every man accommodate himself to others. But he who breaks this law, may be called useless, and troublesome. Yet Cicero opposeth inhumanity to this usefulness, as having regard to this very law.

10. The fifth precept of the law of nature is, that we must forgive him who repents and asks pardon for what is past,

having first taken caution for the time to come. The pardon of what is past, or the remission of an offence, is nothing else but the granting of peace to him that asketh it, after he hath warred against us, and now is become penitent. But peace granted to him that repents not, that is, to him that retains an hostile mind, or that gives not caution for the future, that is, seeks not peace, but opportunity, is not properly peace but fear, and therefore is not commanded by nature. Now to him that will not pardon the penitent, and that gives future caution, peace itself it seems is not pleasing; which is contrary to the natural law.

11. The sixth precept of the natural law is, that in revenge and punishments we must have our eye not at the evil past, but the future good; that is, it is not lawful to inflict punishment for any other end, but that the offender may be corrected, or that others warned by his punishment may become better. But this is confirmed chiefly from hence, that each man is bound by the law of nature to forgive one another, provided he give caution for the future, as hath been showed in the foregoing article. Furthermore, because revenge, if the time past be only considered, is nothing else but a certain triumph, and glory of mind, which points at no end, (for it contemplates only what is past, but the end is a thing to come) but that which is directed to no end, is vain: that revenge therefore which regards not the future, proceeds from vain glory, and is therefore without reason. But to hurt another without reason introduces a war, and is contrary to the fundamental law of nature. It is therefore a precept of the law of nature, that in revenge we look not backwards but forward. Now the breach of this law is commonly called cruelty.

12. But because all signs of hatred and contempt provoke most of all to brawling and fighting, insomuch as most men would rather lose their lives (that I say not, their peace) than

suffer slander, it follows in the seventh place, that it is prescribed by the law of nature, that no man, either by deeds or
words, countenance or laughter, do declare himself to hate or
scorn another. The breach of which law is called reproach. But
although nothing be more frequent than the scoffs and jeers of
the powerful against the weak, and namely, of judges against
guilty persons, which neither relate to the offence of the guilty,
nor the duty of the judges, yet these kind of men do act against
the law of nature, and are to be esteemed for contumelious.

13. The question whether of two men be the more worthy,
belongs not to the natural, but civil state. For it hath been
showed before (Chap. 1. Art. 3) that all men by nature are
equal, and therefore the inequality which now is, suppose
from riches, power, nobility of kindred, is come from the civil
law. I know that Aristotle, in his first book of Politics, affirms
as a foundation of the whole political science, that some men
by nature are made worthy to command, others only to serve;
as if lord and servant were distinguished not by consent of
men, but by an aptness, that is, a certain kind of natural
knowledge or ignorance. Which foundation is not only against
reason (as but now hath been showed) but also against experience. For neither almost is any man so dull of understanding
as not to judge it better to be ruled by himself, than to yield
himself to the government of another; neither if the wiser
and stronger do contest, have these ever or after the upper
hand of those. Whether therefore men be equal by nature, the
equality is to be acknowledged, or whether unequal, because
they are like to contest for dominion, it is necessary for the
obtaining of peace, that they be esteemed as equal; and therefore it is in the eighth place a precept of the law of nature, that
every man be accounted by nature equal to another, the contrary
to which law is pride.

14. As it was necessary to the conservation of each man,

that he should part with some of his rights, so it is no less necessary to the same conservation, that he retain some others, to wit, the right of bodily protection, of free enjoyment of air, water, and all necessaries for life. Since therefore many common rights are retained by those who enter into a peaceable state, and that many peculiar ones are also acquired, hence ariseth this ninth dictate of the natural law, to wit, that what rights soever any man challenges to himself, he also grant the same as due to all the rest; otherwise he frustrates the equality acknowledged in the former article. For what is it else to acknowledge an equality of persons in the making up of society, but to attribute equal right and power to those whom no reason would else engage to enter into society? But to ascribe equal things to equals, is the same with giving things proportional to proportionals. The observation of this law is called meekness, the violation πλεονεξìα; the breakers by the Latins are styled *immodici et immodesti*.

15. In the tenth place it is commanded by the law of nature, that every man in dividing right to others, shew himself equal to either party. By the foregoing law we are forbidden to assume more right by nature to ourselves, than we grant to others. We may take less if we will, for that sometimes is an argument of modesty. But if at any time matter of right be to be divided by us unto others, we are forbidden by this law to favour one more or less than another. For he that by favouring one before another observes not this natural equality, reproaches him whom he thus undervalues: but it is declared above, that a reproach is against the laws of nature. The observance of this precept is called equity; the breach, respect of persons. The Greeks in one word term it προσωποληψìα.

16. From the foregoing law is collected this eleventh, those things which cannot be divided, must be used in common (if they can) and (that the quantity of the matter permit) every

man as much as he lists, but if the quantity permit not, then with limitation, and proportionally to the number of the users. For otherwise that equality can by no means be observed, which we have showed in the foregoing article to be commanded by the law of nature.

17. Also what cannot be divided, nor had in common, it is provided by the law of nature (which may be the twelfth precept) that the use of that thing be either by turns, or adjudged to one only by lot, and that in the using it by turns, it be also decided by lot who shall have the first use of it. For here also regard is to be had unto equality: but no other can be found, but that of lot.

18. But all lot is twofold, arbitrary or natural. Arbitrary is that which is cast by the consent of the contenders, and it consists in mere chance (as they say) or fortune. Natural is primogeniture (in Greek κληρονομία, as it were given by lot) or first possession. Therefore the things which can neither be divided, nor had in common, must be granted to the first possessor; as also those things which belonged to the father are due to the son, unless the father himself have formerly conveyed away that right to some other. Let this therefore stand for the thirteenth law of nature.

19. The fourteenth precept of the law of nature is, that safety must be assured to the mediators for peace. For the reason which commands the end, commands also the means necessary to the end. But the first dictate of reason is peace; all the rest are means to obtain it, and without which peace cannot be had. But neither can peace be had without mediation, nor mediation without safety. It is therefore a dictate of reason, that is, a law of nature, that we must give all security to the mediators for peace.

20. Furthermore, because, although men should agree to make all these and whatsoever other laws of nature, and should

endeavour to keep them, yet doubts and controversies would daily arise concerning the application of them unto their actions, to wit, whether what was done, were against the law or not, (which we call the question of right); whence will follow a fight between parties, either sides supposing themselves wronged; it is therefore necessary to the preservation of peace (because in this case no other fit remedy can possibly be thought on) that both the disagreeing parties refer the matter unto some third, and oblige themselves by mutual compacts to stand to his judgment in deciding the controversy. And he to whom they thus refer themselves is called an arbiter. It is therefore the fifteenth precept of the natural law, that both parties disputing concerning the matter of right submit themselves unto the opinion and judgment of some third.

21. But from this ground, that an arbiter or judge is chosen by the differing parties to determine the controversy, we gather that the arbiter must not be one of the parties. For every man is presumed to seek what is good for himself naturally, and what is just, only for peace's sake, and accidentally; and there. fore cannot observe that same equality commanded by the law of nature so exactly as a third man would do. It is therefore in the sixteenth place contained in the law of nature, that no man must be judge or arbiter in his own cause.

22. From the same ground follows in the seventeenth place, that no man must be judge who propounds unto himself any hope of profit, or glory, from the victory of either part: for the like reason sways here, as in the foregoing law.

23. But when there is some controversy of the fact itself, to wit, whether that be done or not, which is said to be done, the natural law wills that the arbiter trust both parties alike, that is, (because they affirm contradictories) that he believe neither. He must therefore give credit to a third, or a third and fourth, or more, that he may be able to give judgment to

the fact, as often as by other signs he cannot come to the knowledge of it. The eighteenth law of nature therefore enjoins arbiters and judges of fact, that where firm and certain signs of the fact appear not, there they rule their sentence by such witnesses, as seem to be indifferent to both parts.

24. From the above declared definition of an arbiter may be furthermore understood, that no contract or promise must pass between him and the parties whose judge he is appointed, by virtue whereof he may be engaged to speak in favour of either part, nay, or be obliged to judge according to equity, or to pronounce such sentence as he shall truly judge to be equal. The judge is indeed bound to give such sentence as he shall judge to be equal, by the law of nature recounted in the 15th article. To the obligation of which law nothing can be added by way of compact. Such compact therefore would be in vain. Besides, if giving wrong judgment, he should contend for the equity of it, except such compact be of no force, the controversy would remain after judgment given, which is contrary to the constitution of an arbiter, who is so chosen, as both parties have obliged themselves to stand to the judgment which he should pronounce. The law of nature therefore commands the judge to be disengaged, which is its nineteenth precept.

25. Furthermore, forasmuch as the laws of nature are nought else but the dictates of reason, so as, unless a man endeavour to preserve the faculty of right reasoning, he cannot observe the laws of nature, it is manifest, that he who knowingly, or willingly, doth aught whereby the rational faculty may be destroyed or weakened, he knowingly, and willingly, breaks the law of nature. For there is no difference between a man who performs not his duty, and him who does such things willingly, as make it impossible for him to do it. But they destroy and weaken the reasoning faculty, who do that which disturbs

the mind from its natural state; that which most manifestly happens to drunkards and gluttons. We therefore sin, in the twentieth place, against the law of nature by drunkenness.

26. Perhaps some man, who sees all these precepts of nature derived by a certain artifice from the single dictate of reason advising us to look to the preservation and safeguard of ourselves, will say that the deduction of these laws is so hard, that it is not to be expected they will be vulgarly known, and therefore neither will they prove obliging: for laws, if they be not known, oblige not, nay, indeed are not laws. To this I answer, it is true, that hope, fear, anger, ambition, covetousness, vain glory, and other perturbations of mind, do hinder a man so, as he cannot attain to the knowledge of these laws, whilst those passions prevail in him: but there is no man who is not sometimes in a quiet mind. At that time therefore there is nothing easier for him to know, though he be never so rude and unlearned, than this only rule, that when he doubts, whether what he is now doing to another, may be done by the law of nature, or not, he conceive himself to be in that other's stead. Here instantly those perturbations which persuaded him to the fact, being now cast into the other scale, dissuade him as much. And this rule is not only easy, but is anciently celebrated in these words, *quod tibi fieri non vis, alteri ne feceris:* do not that to others, you would not have done to yourself.

27. But because most men, by reason of their perverse desire of present profit, are very unapt to observe these laws, although acknowledged by them; if perhaps some more humble than the rest should exercise that equity and usefulness which reason dictates, those not practising the same, surely they would not follow reason in so doing; nor would they hereby procure themselves peace, but a more certain quick destruction, and the keepers of the law become a mere prey to the breakers of it. It is not therefore to be imagined, that by nature, (that is, by

reason) men are obliged to the exercise of all these laws * in that state of men wherein they are not practised by others. We are obliged yet in the interim to a readiness of mind to observe them whensoever their observation shall seem to conduce to the end for which they were ordained. We must therefore conclude, that the law of nature doth always and everywhere oblige in the internal court, or that of conscience, but not always in the external court, but then only when it may be done with safety.

28. But the laws which oblige conscience, may be broken by an act, not only contrary to them, but also agreeable with them, if so be that he who does it be of another opinion. For though the act itself be answerable to the laws, yet his conscience is against them.

29. The laws of nature are immutable and eternal: what they forbid, can never be lawful; what they command, can never be unlawful. For pride, ingratitude, breach of contracts (or injury), inhumanity, contumely, will never be lawful, nor the contrary virtues to these ever unlawful, as we take them for dispositions of the mind, that is, as they are considered in the

* Nay, among these laws some things there are, the omission whereof (provided it be done for peace or self-preservation) seems rather to be the fulfilling, than breach of the natural law. For he that doth all things against those that do all things, and plunders plunderers, doth equity; but on the other side, to do that which in peace is a handsome action, and becoming an honest man, is dejectedness, and poorness of spirit, and a betraying of one's self, in the time of war. But there are certain natural laws, whose exercise ceaseth not even in the time of war itself; for I cannot understand what drunkenness, or cruelty (that is, revenge which respects not the future good) can advance toward peace, or the preservation of any man. Briefly, in the state of nature, what is just, and unjust, is not to be esteemed by the actions, but by the counsel and conscience, of the actor. That which is done out of necessity, out of endeavour for peace, for the preservation of ourselves, is done with right; otherwise every damage done to a man would be a breach of the natural law, and an injury against God.

court of conscience, where only they oblige, and are laws. Yet actions may be so diversified by circumstances, and the civil law, that what is done with equity at one time, is guilty of iniquity at another; and what suits with reason at one time, is contrary to it another. Yet reason is still the same, and changeth not her end, which is peace, and defence; nor the means to attain them, to wit, those virtues of the mind which we have declared above, and which cannot be abrogated by any custom or law whatsoever.

30. It is evident by what hath hitherto been said, how easily the laws of nature are to be observed, because they require the endeavour only, (but that must be true and constant); which whoso shall perform, we may rightly call him just. For he who tends to this with his whole might, namely, that his actions be squared according to the precepts of nature, he shows clearly that he hath a mind to fulfil all those laws; which is all we are obliged to by rational nature. Now he that hath done all he is obliged to, is a just man.

31. All writers do agree that the natural law is the same with the moral. Let us see wherefore this is true. We must know, therefore, that good and evil are names given to things to signify the inclination or aversion of them by whom they were given. But the inclinations of men are diverse, according to their diverse constitutions, customs, opinions; as we may see in those things we apprehend by sense, as by tasting, touching, smelling; but much more in those which pertain to the common actions of life, where what this man commends, (that is to say, calls good) the other undervalues, as being evil; nay, very often the same man at diverse times praises and dispraises the same thing. Whilst thus they do, necessary it is there should be discord and strife. They are therefore so long in the state of war, as by reason of the diversity of the present appetites, they mete good and evil by diverse measures. All

men easily acknowledge this state, as long as they are in it, to be evil, and by consequence that peace is good. They therefore who could not agree concerning a present, do agree concerning a future good, which indeed is a work of reason; for things present are obvious to the sense, things to come to our reason only. Reason declaring peace to be good, it follows by the same reason, that all the necessary means to peace be good also; and therefore that modesty, equity, trust, humanity, mercy, (which we have demonstrated to be necessary to peace), are good manners or habits, that is, virtues. The law therefore, in the means to peace, commands also good manners, or the practice of virtue: and therefore it is called moral.

32. But because men cannot put off this same irrational appetite, whereby they greedily prefer the present good (to which, by strict consequence, many unforeseen evils do adhere) before the future, it happens, that though all men do agree in the commendation of the foresaid virtues, yet they disagree still concerning their nature, to wit, in which each of them doth consist. For as oft as another's good action displeaseth any man, that action hath the name given of some neighbouring vice; likewise the bad actions, which please them, are ever entitled to some virtue. Whence it comes to pass that the same action is praised by these, and called virtue, and dispraised by those, and termed vice. Neither is there as yet any remedy found by philosophers for this matter; for since they could not observe the goodness of actions to consist in this, that it was in order to peace, and the evil in this, that it related to discord, they built a moral philosophy wholly estranged from the moral law, and unconstant to itself. For they would have the nature of virtues seated in a certain kind of mediocrity between two extremes, and the vices in the extremes themselves; which is apparently false. For to dare is commended, and, under the name of fortitude is taken for a virtue, although it

be an extreme, if the cause be approved. Also the quantity of a thing given, whether it be great, or little, or between both, makes not liberality, but the cause of giving it. Neither is it injustice, if I give any man more, of what is mine own, than I owe him. The laws of nature therefore are the sum of moral philosophy, whereof I have only delivered such precepts in this place, as appertain to the preservation of ourselves against those dangers which arise from discord. But there are other precepts of rational nature, from whence spring other virtues; for temperance also is a precept of reason, because intemperance tends to sickness and death. And so fortitude too, that is, that same faculty of resisting stoutly in present dangers, (and which are more hardly declined than overcome) because it is a means tending to the preservation of him that resists.

33. But those which we call the laws of nature, (since they are nothing else but certain conclusions understood by reason, of things to be done and omitted; but a law, to speak properly and accurately, is the speech of him who by right commands somewhat to others to be done or omitted), are not (in propriety of speech) laws, as they proceed from nature. Yet, as they are delivered by God in holy Scriptures, (as we shall see in the chapter following) they are most properly called by the name of laws: for the sacred Scripture is the speech of God commanding over all things by greatest right.

CHAPTER IV

THAT THE LAW OF NATURE IS A DIVINE LAW

(The text of this chapter is omitted.)

Part II: DOMINION

CHAPTER V

OF THE CAUSES AND FIRST BEGINNING OF CIVIL GOVERNMENT

1. IT is of itself manifest, that the actions of men proceed from the will, and the will from hope and fear, insomuch as when they shall see a greater good, or less evil, likely to happen to them by the breach, than observation of the laws, they will wittingly violate them. The hope therefore which each man hath of his security and self-preservation, consists in this, that by force or craft he may disappoint his neighbour, either openly, or by stratagem. Whence we may understand, that the natural laws, though well understood, do not instantly secure any man in their practice, and consequently, that as long as there is no caution had from the invasion of others, there remains to every man that same primitive right of self-defence, by such means as either he can or will make use of, that is, a right to all things, or the right of war. And it is sufficient for the fulfilling of the natural law, that a man be prepared in mind to embrace peace when it may be had.

2. It is a fond saying, that all laws are silent in the time of war, and it is a true one, not only if we speak of the civil, but also of the natural laws, provided they be referred not to the mind, but to the actions of men, by chap. iii. art. 27. And we mean such a war as is of all men against all men; such as is the mere state of nature; although in the war of nation against nation a certain mean was wont to be observed. And therefore in old time there was a manner of living, and as it were a certain economy, which they called ληστρικὴν, living by rapine, which was neither against the law of nature (things

then so standing), nor void of glory to those who exercised it with valour, not with cruelty. Their custom was, taking away the rest, to spare life, and abstain from oxen fit for plough, and every instrument serviceable to husbandry, which yet is not so to be taken, as if they were bound to do thus by the law of nature, but that they had regard to their own glory herein, lest by too much cruelty, they might be suspected guilty of fear.

3. Since therefore the exercise of the natural law is necessary for the preservation of peace, and that for the exercise of the natural law security is no less necessary, it is worth the considering what that is which affords such a security. For this matter nothing else can be imagined, but that each man provide himself of such meet helps, as the invasion of one on the other may be rendered so dangerous, as either of them may think it better to refrain, than to meddle. But first, it is plain, that the consent of two or three cannot make good such a security; because that the addition but of one, or some few on the other side, is sufficient to make the victory undoubtedly sure, and heartens the enemy to attack us. It is therefore necessary, to the end the security sought for may be obtained, that the number of them who conspire in a mutual assistance be so great, that the accession of some few to the enemy's party may not prove to them a matter of moment sufficient to assure the victory.

4. Furthermore, how great soever the number of them is who meet on self-defence, if yet they agree not among themselves of some excellent means whereby to compass this, but every man after his own manner shall make use of his endeavours, nothing will be done; because that, divided in their opinions, they will be a hindrance to each other, or if they agree well enough to some one action through hope of victory, spoil, or revenge, yet afterward through diversity of wits, and counsels, or emulation, and envy, with which men naturally

contend, they will be so torn and rent, as they will neither give mutual help, nor desire peace, except they be constrained to it by some common fear. Whence it follows that the consent of many, (which consists in this only, as we have already defined in the foregoing section, that they direct all their actions to the same end, and the common good), that is to say, that the society proceeding from mutual help only, yields not that security which they seek for, who meet and agree in the exercise of the above-named laws of nature; but that somewhat else must be done, that those who have once consented for the common good, to peace and mutual help, may by fear be restrained, lest afterwards they again dissent, when their private interest shall appear discrepant from the common good.

5. Aristotle reckons among those animals which he calls politic, not man only, but divers others; as the ant, the bee, &c., which, though they be destitute of reason, by which they may contract and submit to government, notwithstanding by consenting, (that is to say) ensuing or eschewing the same things, they so direct their actions to a common end, that their meetings are not obnoxious unto any seditions. Yet is not their gathering together a civil government, and therefore those animals not to be termed political, because their government is only a consent, or many wills concurring in one object, not (as is necessary in civil government) one will. It is very true that in those creatures, living only by sense and appetite, their consent of minds is so durable, as there is no need of anything more to secure it, and (by consequence) to preserve peace among them, than barely their natural inclination. But among men the case is otherwise. For, first, among them there is a contestation of honour and preferment; among beasts there is none: whence hatred and envy, out of which arise sedition and war, is among men; among beasts no such matter. Next, the natural appetite of bees, and the like creatures, is conformable,

and they desire the common good which among them differs not from their private. But <u>man scarce esteems anything good which hath not somewhat of eminence in the enjoyment, more than that which others do possess.</u> Thirdly, those creatures which are void of reason, see no defect, or think they see none, in the administration of their commonweals; but in a multitude of men there are many who, supposing themselves wiser than others, endeavour to innovate, and divers innovators innovate divers ways, which is a mere distraction, and civil war. Fourthly, these brute creatures, howsoever they may have the use of their voice to signify their affections to each other, yet want they that same art of words which is necessarily required to those motions in the mind, whereby good is represented to it as being better, and evil as worse than in truth it is. But the tongue of man is a trumpet of war and sedition: and it is reported of Pericles, that he sometimes by his elegant speeches thundered, and lightened, and confounded whole Greece itself. Fifthly, they cannot distinguish between injury and harm; thence it happens that as long as it is well with them, they blame not their fellows. But those men are of most trouble to the republic, who have most leisure to be idle; for they use not to contend for public places before they have gotten the victory over hunger and cold. Last of all, the consent of those brutal creatures is natural, that of men by compact only, that is to say, artificial. It is therefore no matter of wonder if somewhat more be needful for men to the end they may live in peace. <u>Wherefore consent or contracted society, without some common power whereby particular men may be ruled through fear of punishment, doth not suffice to make up that security which is requisite to the exercise of natural justice.</u>

6. <u>Since therefore the conspiring of many wills to the same end doth not suffice to preserve peace, and to make a lasting defence, it is requisite that, in those necessary matters which</u>

concern peace and self-defence, there be but one will of all men. But this cannot be done, unless every man will so subject his will to some other one, to wit, either man or council, that whatsoever his will is in those things which are necessary to the common peace, it be received for the wills of all men in general, and of every one in particular. Now the gathering together of many men who deliberate of what is to be done, or not to be done, for the common good of all men, is that which I call a council.

7. This submission of the wills of all those men to the will of one man, or one council, is then made, when each one of them obligeth himself by contract to every one of the rest, not to resist the will of that one man, or council, to which he hath submitted himself; that is, that he refuse him not the use of his wealth and strength against any others whatsoever (for he is supposed still to retain a right of defending himself against violence) and this is called union. But we understand that to be the will of the council, which is the will of the major part of those men of whom the council consists.

8. But though the will itself be not voluntary, but only the beginning of voluntary actions (for we will not to will, but to act) and therefore falls least of all under deliberation and compact; yet he who submits his will to the will of another, conveys to that other the right of his strength and faculties; insomuch as when the rest have done the same, he to whom they have submitted hath so much power, as by the terror of it he can conform the wills of particular men unto unity and concord.

9. Now union thus made is called a city, or civil society, and also a civil person; for when there is one will of all men, it is to be esteemed for one person, and by the word one it is to be known, and distinguished from all particular men, as having its own rights and properties. Insomuch as neither any one

citizen, nor all of them together, (if we except him whose will stands for the will of all) is to be accounted the city. A city therefore (that we may define it) is one person, whose will, by the compact of many men, is to be received for the will of them all; so as he may use all the power and faculties of each particular person, to the maintenance of peace, and for common defence.

10. But although every city be a civil person, yet every civil person is not a city; for it may happen that many citizens, by the permission of the city, may join together in one person, for the doing of certain things. These now will be civil persons, as the companies of merchants, and many other convents; but cities they are not, because they have not submitted themselves to the will of the company simply, and in all things, but in certain things only determined by the city, and on such terms as it is lawful for any one of them to contend in judgment against the body itself of the sodality; which is by no means allowable to a citizen against the city. Such like societies, therefore, are civil persons subordinate to the city.

11. In every city, that man or council, to whose will each particular man hath subjected his will (so as hath been declared) is said to have the supreme power, or chief command, or dominion; which power and right of commanding, consists in this, that each citizen hath conveyed all his strength and power to that man or council; which to have done (because no man can transfer his power in a natural manner) is nothing else than to have parted with his right of resisting. Each citizen, as also every subordinate civil person, is called the subject of him who hath the chief command.

12. By what hath been said, it is sufficiently showed, in what manner, and by what degrees, many natural persons, through desire of preserving themselves, and by mutual fear, have grown together into a civil person, whom we have called

a city. But they who submit themselves to another for fear,
either submit to him whom they fear, or some other whom
they confide in for protection. They act according to the first
manner who are vanquished in war, that they may not be
slain; they according to the second, who are not yet overcome,
that they may not be overcome. The first manner receives its
beginning from natural power, and may be called the natural
beginning of a city; the latter from the council and constitution of those who meet together, which is a beginning by institution. Hence it is that there are two kinds of cities, the
one natural, such as is the paternal and despotical; the other
institutive, which may be also called political. In the first, the
lord acquires to himself such citizens as he will; in the other,
the citizens by their own wills appoint a lord over themselves,
whether he be one man, or one company of men, endued with
the command in chief. But we will speak, in the first place, of
a city political or by institution; and next, of a city natural.

CHAPTER VI

OF THE RIGHT OF HIM, WHETHER COUNCIL OR ONE MAN ONLY, WHO HATH THE SUPREME POWER IN THE CITY

1. WE must consider first of all what a multitude * of men (gathering themselves of their own free wills into society) is, namely, that it is not any one body, but many men, whereof each one hath his own will and his peculiar judgment concerning all things that may be proposed. And though by particular contracts each single man may have his own right and propriety, so as one may say *this is mine,* the other, *that is his;* yet will there not be anything of which the whole multitude, as a person distinct from a single man, can rightly say, this is mine, more than another's. Neither must we ascribe any action to the multitude, as its own, but (if all or more of them do agree) it will not be an action, but as many actions as men.

* The doctrine of the power of a city over its citizens, almost wholly depends on the understanding of the difference which is between a multitude of men ruling, and a multitude ruled. For such is the nature of a city, that a multitude or company of citizens not only may have command, but may also be subject to command; but in diverse senses. Which difference I did believe was clearly enough explained in the first article; but by the objections of many against those things which follow, I discern otherwise. Wherefore it seemed good to me, to the end I might make a fuller explication, to add these few things.

By multitude, because it is a collective word, we understand more than one, so as a multitude of men is the same with many men. The same word, because it is of the singular number, signifies one thing, namely, one multitude. But in neither sense can a multitude be understood to have one will given to it by nature, but to either a several; and therefore neither is any one action whatsoever to be attributed to it. Wherefore a multitude cannot promise, contract, acquire right, convey right, act, have, possess, and the like, unless it be every one apart, and

For although in some great sedition, it is commonly said, that the people of that city have taken up arms; yet is it true of those only who are in arms, or who consent to them. For the city, which is one person, cannot take up arms against itself. Whatsoever therefore is done by the multitude, must be understood to be done by every one of those by whom it is made up; and that he, who being in the multitude, and yet consented not, nor gave any helps to the things that were done by it, must be judged to have done nothing. Besides, in a multitude not yet reduced into one person, in that manner as hath been said, there remains that same state of nature in which all things belong to all men, and there is no place for *meum* and *tuum,* which is called dominion and propriety, by reason that that security is not yet extant which we have declared above to be necessarily requisite for the practice of the natural laws.

2. Next, we must consider that every one of the multitude (by whose means there may be a beginning to make up the city) must agree with the rest, that in those matters which shall be propounded by any one in the assembly, that he received for the will of all which the major part shall approve of; for

---

man by man; so as there must be as many promises, compacts, rights, and actions, as men. Wherefore a multitude is no natural person. But if the same multitude do contract one with another, that the will of one man, or the agreeing wills of the major part of them, shall be received for the will of all, then it becomes one person. For it is endued with a will, and therefore can do voluntary actions, such as are commanding, making laws, acquiring and transferring of right, and so forth; and it is oftener called the people, than the multitude. We must therefore distinguish thus. When we say the people or multitude wills, commands, or doth anything, it is understood that the city which commands, wills and acts by the will of one, or the concurring wills of more, which cannot be done, but in an assembly. But as oft as anything is said to be done by a multitude of men, whether great or small, without the will of that man or assembly of men, that is understood to be done by a subjected people, that is, by many single citizens together, and not proceeding from one will, but from diverse wills of diverse men, who are citizens and subjects, but not a city.

otherwise there will be no will at all of a multitude of men, whose wills and votes differ so variously. Now if any one will not consent, the rest notwithstanding shall among themselves constitute the city without him. Whence it will come to pass, that the city retains its primitive right against the dissenter, that is, the right of war, as against an enemy.

3. But because we said in the foregoing chapter, the sixth article, that there was required to the security of men, not only their consent, but also the subjection of their wills in such things as were necessary to peace and defence; and that in that union and subjection the nature of a city consisted; we must discern now in this place, out of those things which may be propounded, discussed, and stated in an assembly of men, (all whose wills are contained in the will of the major part) what things are necessary to peace and common defence. But first of all, it is necessary to peace, that a man be so far forth protected against the violence of others, that he may live securely, that is, that he may have no just cause to fear others, so long as he doth them no injury. Indeed, to make men altogether safe from mutual harms, so as they cannot be hurt or injuriously killed, is impossible; and, therefore, comes not within deliberation. But care may be had, there be no just cause of fear; for security is the end wherefore men submit themselves to others, which if it be not had, no man is supposed to have submitted himself to aught, or to have quitted his right to all things, before that there was a care had of his security.

4. It is not enough to obtain this security, that every one of those who are now growing up into a city, do covenant with the rest, either by words or writing, not to steal, not to kill, and to observe the like laws; for the pravity of human disposition is manifest to all, and by experience too well known how little (removing the punishment) men are kept to their duties, through conscience of their promises. We must therefore

provide for our security, not by compacts, but by punishments; and there is then sufficient provision made, when there are so great punishments appointed for every injury, as apparently it prove a greater evil to have done it, than not to have done it. For all men, by a necessity of nature, choose that which to them appears to be the less evil.

5. Now the right of punishing is then understood to be given to any one, when every man contracts not to assist him who is to be punished. But I will call this right, the sword of justice. But these kind of contracts men observe well enough, for the most part, till either themselves or their near friends are to suffer.

6. Because therefore for the security of particular men, and, by consequence, for the common peace, it is necessary that the right of using the sword for punishment be transferred to some man or council, that man or council is necessarily understood by right to have the supreme power in the city. For he that by right punisheth at his own discretion, by right compels all men to all things which he himself wills; than which a greater command cannot be imagined.

7. But in vain do they worship peace at home, who cannot defend themselves against foreigners; neither is it possible for them to protect themselves against foreigners, whose forces are not united. And therefore it is necessary for the preservation of particulars, that there be some one council or one man, who hath the right to arm, to gather together, to unite so many citizens, in all dangers and on all occasions, as shall be needful for common defence against the certain number and strength of the enemy; and again, (as often as he shall find it expedient) to make peace with them. We must understand therefore, that particular citizens have conveyed their whole right of war and peace, unto some one man or council; and that this right (which we may call the sword of war) belongs to the

same man or council, to whom the sword of justice belongs. For no man can by right compel citizens to take up arms, and be at the expenses of war, but he who by right can punish him who doth not obey. Both swords therefore, as well this of war, as that of justice, even by the constitution itself of a city, and essentially, do belong to the chief command.

8. But because the right of the sword is nothing else but to have power by right to use the sword at his own will, it follows, that the judgment of its right use pertains to the same party: for if the power of judging were in one, and the power of executing in another, nothing would be done. For in vain would he give judgment, who could not execute his commands, or, if he executed them by the power of another, he himself is not said to have the power of the sword, but that other, to whom he is only an officer. All judgment therefore in a city belongs to him who hath the swords, that is, to him who hath the supreme authority.

9. Furthermore, since it no less, nay, it much more conduceth to peace, to prevent brawls from arising, than to appease them being risen; and that all controversies are bred from hence, that the opinions of men differ concerning *meum* and *tuum,* just and unjust, profitable and unprofitable, good and evil, honest and dishonest, and the like, which every man esteems according to his own judgment; it belongs to the same chief power to make some common rules for all men, and to declare them publicly, by which every man may know what may be called his, what another's, what just, what unjust, what honest, what dishonest, what good, what evil, that is summarily, what is to be done, what to be avoided in our common course of life. But those rules and measures are usually called the civil laws, or the laws of the city, as being the commands of him who hath the supreme power in the city. And the civil laws (that we may define them) are nothing else

but the commands of him who hath the chief authority in the city, for direction of the future actions of his citizens.

10. Furthermore, since the affairs of the city, both those of war and peace, cannot possibly be all administered by one man, or one council, without officers and subordinate magistrates, and that it appertaineth to peace, and common defence, that they to whom it belongs justly to judge of controversies, to search into neighbouring councils, prudently to wage war, and on all hands warily to attend the benefit of the city, should also rightly exercise their offices; it is consonant to reason, that they depend on, and be chosen by him who hath the chief command both in war and in peace.

11. It is also manifest, that all voluntary actions have their beginning from, and necessarily depend on the will, and that the will of doing, or omitting aught, depends on the opinion of the good and evil of the reward or punishment, which a man conceives he shall receive by the act or omission; so as the actions of all men are ruled by the opinions of each; wherefore, by evident and necessary inference, we may understand that it very much concerns the interest of peace, that no opinions or doctrines be delivered to citizens, by which they may imagine, that either by right they may not obey the laws of the city, that is, the commands of that man or council, to whom the supreme power is committed, or that it is lawful to resist him, or that a less punishment remains for him that denies, than him that yields obedience. For if one command somewhat to be done under penalty of natural death, another forbid it under pain of eternal death, and both by their own right, it will follow that the citizens, although innocent, are not only by right punishable, but that the city itself is altogether dissolved; for no man can serve two masters: nor is he less, but rather more, a master, whom we believe we are to obey for fear of damnation, than he whom we obey for fear

of temporal death. It follows therefore that this one, whether man or court, to whom the city hath committed the supreme power, have also this right; that he both judge what opinions * and doctrines are enemies unto peace, and also that he forbid them to be taught.

12. Last of all, from this consideration, that each citizen hath submitted his will to his who hath the supreme command in the city, so as he may not employ his strength against him; it follows manifestly, that whatsoever shall be done by him who commands, must not be punished. For as he who hath

* There is scarce any principle, neither in the worship of God, nor human sciences, from whence there may not spring dissensions, discords, reproaches, and by degrees war itself. Neither doth this happen by reason of the falsehood of the principle, but of the disposition of men, who, seeming wise to themselves, will needs appear such to all others. But though such dissensions cannot be hindered from arising, yet may they be restrained by the exercise of the supreme power, that they prove no hindrance to the public peace. Of these kinds of opinions therefore I have not spoken in this place. There are certain doctrines wherewith subjects being tainted, they verily believe that obedience may be refused to the city, and that by right they may, nay ought, to oppose and fight against chief princes and dignities. Such are those which, whether directly and openly, or more obscurely and by consequence, require obedience to be given to others beside them to whom the supreme authority is committed. I deny not, but this reflects on that power which many living under other government, ascribe to the chief head of the Church of Rome, and also on that which elsewhere, out of that Church, bishops require in theirs to be given to them; and last of all, on that liberty which the lower sort of citizens, under pretence of religion, do challenge to themselves. For what civil war was there ever in the Christian world, which did not either grow from, or was nourished by this root? The judgment therefore of doctrines, whether they be repugnant to civil obedience or not, and if they be repugnant, the power of prohibiting them to be taught, I do here attribute to the civil authority. For since there is no man who grants not to the city the judgment of those things which belong to its peace and defence, and it is manifest that the opinions which I have already recited do relate to its peace, it follows necessarily, that the examination of those opinions, whether they be such or not, must be referred to the city, that is, to him who hath the supreme authority.

not power enough, cannot punish him naturally; so neither can
he punish him by right, who by right hath not sufficient power.

13. It is most manifest by what hath been said, that in every
perfect city (that is, where no citizen hath right to use his
faculties, at his own discretion, for the preservation of himself,
or where the right of the private sword is excluded) there is a
supreme power in some one, greater than which cannot by
right be conferred by men, or greater than which no mortal
man can have over himself. But that power, greater than which
cannot by men be conveyed on a man, we call absolute.* For

---

* A popular state openly challengeth absolute dominion, and the citizens
oppose it not. For in the gathering together of many men, they acknowledge the face of a city; and even the unskilful understand, that matters
there are ruled by council. Yet monarchy is no less a city than democracy;
and absolute kings have their counsellors, from whom they will take
advice, and suffer their power, in matters of greater consequence, to be
guided, but not recalled. But it appears not to most men how a city is
contained in the person of a king; and therefore they object against
absolute command: first, that if any man had such a right, the condition of the citizens would be miserable. For thus they think, he will
take all, spoil all, kill all; and every man counts it his only happiness
that he is not already spoiled and killed. But why should he do thus?
Not because he can; for unless he have a mind to it, he will not do it.
Will he, to please one, or some few, spoil all the rest? First, though by
right, that is, without injury to them, he may do it, yet can he not do it
justly, that is, without breach of the natural laws, and injury against
God. And therefore there is some security for subjects in the oaths which
princes take. Next, if he could justly do it, or that he made no account
of his oath, yet appears there no reason why he should desire it, since
he finds no good in it. But it cannot be denied but a prince may sometimes have an inclination to do wickedly; but grant then, that thou
hadst given him a power which were not absolute, but so much only as
sufficed to defend thee from the injuries of others, which, if thou wilt
be safe, is necessary for thee to give; are not all the same things to be
feared? For he that hath strength enough to protect all, wants not suf-
ficiency to oppress all. Here is no other difficulty then, but that human
affairs cannot be without some inconvenience. And this inconvenience
itself is in the citizens, not in the government. For if men could rule
themselves, every man by his own command, that is to say, could they
live according to the laws of nature, there would be no need at all of a

whosoever hath so submitted his will to the will of the city, that he can, unpunished, do any thing, make laws, judge controversies, set penalties, make use, at his own pleasure, of the strength and wealth of men, and all this by right, truly he hath given him the greatest dominion that can be granted. This same may be confirmed by experience in all the cities which are or ever have been; for though it be sometimes in doubt, what man or council hath the chief command, yet ever there is such a command, and always exercised, except in the time of sedition and civil war, and then there are two chief commands made out of one. Now, those seditious persons who dispute against absolute authority, do not so much care to destroy it, as to convey it on others; for removing this power, they together take away civil society, and a confusion of all things returns. There is so much obedience joined to this absolute right of the chief ruler, as is necessarily required for the government of the city, that is to say, so much as that right of his may not be granted in vain. Now this kind of obedience, although for some reasons it may sometimes, by right, be denied, yet because a greater cannot be performed, we will call it simple. But the obligation to perform this grows not immediately from that contract, by which we have conveyed all our right on the city, but immediately from hence, that, without obedience, the city's right would be frustrate, and by consequence there would be no city constituted. For it is

---

city, nor of a common coercive power. Secondly, they object, that there is no dominion in the Christian world absolute; which indeed is not true, for all monarchies, and all other states, are so. For although they who have the chief command, do not all those things they would, and what they know profitable to the city, the reason of that is not the defect of right in them, but the consideration of their citizens, who busied about their private interest, and careless of what tends to the public, cannot sometimes be drawn to perform their duties without the hazard of the city. Wherefore princes sometimes forbear the exercise of their right, and prudently remit somewhat of the act, but nothing of their right.

one thing if I say, I give you right to command what you will; another, if I say, I will do whatsoever you command. And the command may be such, as I would rather die than do it. Forasmuch therefore as no man can be bound to will being killed, much less is he tied to that, which to him is worse than death. If therefore I be commanded to kill myself, I am not bound to do it; for though I deny to do it, yet the right of dominion is not frustrated, since others may be found, who being commanded, will not refuse to do it; neither do I refuse to do that which I have contracted to do. In like manner, if the chief ruler command any man to kill him, he is not tied to do it, because it cannot be conceived that he made any such covenant. Nor if he command to execute a parent, whether he be innocent, or guilty, and condemned by the law, since there are others who, being commanded, will do that, and a son will rather die, than live infamous, and hated of all the world. There are many other cases, in which, since the commands are shameful to be done by some, and not by others, obedience may, by right, be performed by these, and refused by those; and this, without breach of that absolute right which was given to the chief ruler. For in no case is the right taken away from him, of slaying those who shall refuse to obey him. But they who thus kill men, although by right, given them from him that hath it, yet if they use that right otherwise than right reason requires, they sin against the laws of nature, that is, against God.

14. Neither can any man give somewhat to himself; for he is already supposed to have what he can give himself. Nor can he be obliged to himself; for the same party being both the obliged and the obliger, and the obliger having power to release the obliged, it were merely in vain for a man to be obliged to himself, because he can release himself at his own pleasure; and he that can do this, is already actually free. Whence it is plain, that the city is not tied to the civil laws; for the civil

laws are the laws of the city, by which, if she were engaged, she should be engaged to herself. Neither can the city be obliged to her citizen, because, if he will, he can free her from her obligation; and he will, as oft as she wills, (for the will of every citizen is in all things comprehended in the will of the city); the city therefore is free when she pleaseth, that is, she is now actually free. But the will of a council, or one who hath the supreme authority given him, is the will of the city: he therefore contains the wills of all particular citizens. Therefore neither is he bound to the civil laws (for this is to be bound to himself) nor to any of his citizens.

15. Now because (as hath been shown above) before the constitution of a city all things belonged to all men, nor is there that thing which any man can so call his, as any other may not, by the same right, claim as his own, (for where all things are common, there can be nothing proper to any man) it follows, that propriety received its beginning * when cities received theirs, and that that only is proper to each man, which he can keep by the laws, and the power of the whole city, that is, of him on whom its chief command is conferred. Whence we understand, that each particular citizen hath a propriety to which none of his fellow-citizens hath right, because they are tied to the same laws; but he hath no propriety in which the chief ruler (whose commands are the laws, whose will contains the will of each man, and who, by every single person, is constituted the supreme judge) hath not a right. But

* What is objected by some, that the propriety of goods, even before the constitution of cities, was found in fathers of families, that objection is vain, because I have already declared, that a family is a little city. For the sons of a family have a propriety of their goods granted them by their father, distinguished indeed from the rest of the sons of the same family, but not from the propriety of the father himself. But the fathers of divers families, who are subject neither to any common father nor lord, have a common right in all things.

although there be many things which the city permits to its citizens, and therefore they may sometimes go to law against their chief; yet is not that action belonging to civil right, but to natural equity; neither is it concerning what * by right he may do who hath the supreme power, but what he hath been willing should be done, and therefore he shall be judge him· self, as though (the equity of the cause being well understood) he could not give wrong judgment.

16. Theft, murder, adultery, and all injuries are forbid by the laws of nature; but what is to be called theft, what murder, what adultery, what injury in a citizen, this is not to be determined by the natural, but by the civil law. For not every taking away of the thing which another possesseth, but only another man's goods, is theft; but what is our's, and what another's, is a question belonging to the civil law. In like manner, not every killing of a man is murder, but only that which the civil law forbids; neither is all encounter with women adultery, but only that which the civil law prohibits. Lastly, all breach of promise is an injury, where the promise itself is lawful; but where there is no right to make any compact, there can be no conveyance of it, and therefore there can no injury follow, as hath been said in the second chapter, Article 17. Now what we may contract for, and what not, depends

* As often as a citizen is granted to have an action of law against the supreme, that is, against the city, the question is not in that action, whether the city may, by right, keep possession of the thing in controversy, but whether by the laws formerly made she would keep it; for the law is the declared will of the supreme. Since then the city may raise money from the citizens under two titles, either as tribute, or as debt, in the former case there is no action of law allowed, for there can be no question whether the city have the right to require tribute; in the latter it is allowed, because the city will take nothing from its citizens by fraud or cunning, and yet if need require, all they have, openly. And therefore he that condemns this place, saying, that by this doctrine it is easy for princes to free themselves from their debts, he does it impertinently.

wholly upon the civil laws. The city of Lacedæmon therefore
rightly ordered that those young men who could so take away
certain goods from others as not to be caught, should go unpunished; for it was nothing else, but to make a law that what
was so acquired should be their own, and not another's.
Rightly also is that man everywhere slain, whom we kill in
war, or by the necessity of self-defence. So also that copulation
which in one city is matrimony, in another will be judged
adultery. Also those contracts which make up marriage in one
citizen, do not so in another, although of the same city; because that he who is forbidden by the city (that is, by that one
man or council whose the supreme power is) to contract aught,
hath no right to make any contract, and therefore having made
any, it is not valid, and by consequence, no marriage. But his
contract which received no prohibition, was therefore of force,
and so was matrimony. Neither adds it any force to any unlawful contracts, that they were made by an oath or sacrament; *
for those add nothing to the strengthening of the contract, as
hath been said above, Chap. 11. Art. 22. What therefore theft,
what murder, what adultery, and in general what injury is,

---

* Whether matrimony be a sacrament (in which sense that word is
used by some divines) or not, it is not my purpose to dispute. Only I say,
that the legitimate contract of a man and woman to live together, that
is, granted by the civil law, whether it be a sacrament or not, is surely
a legitimate marriage; but that copulation which the city hath prohibited
is no marriage, since it is of the essence of marriage to be a legitimate
contract. There were legitimate marriages in many places, as among the
Jews, the Grecians, the Romans, which yet might be dissolved. But with
those who permit no such contracts, but by a law that they shall never
be broke, wedlock cannot be dissolved; and the reason is, because the
city hath commanded it to be indissoluble, not because matrimony is a
sacrament. Wherefore the ceremonies which at weddings are to be performed in the temple, to bless, or (if I may say so) to consecrate the
husband and wife, will perhaps belong only to the office of clergymen;
all the rest, namely, who, when, and by what contracts marriages may
be made, pertains to the laws of the city.

must be known by the civil laws, that is, the commands of him who hath the supreme authority.

17. This same supreme command and absolute power, seems so harsh to the greatest part of men, as they hate the very naming of them; which happens chiefly through want of knowledge, what human nature and the civil laws are, and partly also through their default, who, when they are invested with so great authority, abuse their power to their own lust. That they may therefore avoid this kind of supreme authority, some of them will have a city well enough constituted, if they who shall be the citizens convening, do agree concerning certain articles propounded, and in that convent agitated and approved, and do command them to be observed, and punishments prescribed to be inflicted on them who shall break them. To which purpose, and also to the repelling of a foreign enemy, they appoint a certain and limited return, with this condition, that if that suffice not, they may call a new convention of estates. Who sees not in a city thus constituted, that the assembly who prescribed those things had an absolute power? If therefore the assembly continue, or from time to time have a certain day and place of meeting, that power will be perpetual. But if they wholly dissolve, either the city dissolves with them, and so all is returned to the state of war, or else there is somewhere a power left to punish those who shall transgress the laws, whosoever or how many soever they be that have it, which cannot possibly be without an absolute power. For he that by right hath this might given, by punishments to restrain what citizens he pleaseth, hath such a power as a greater cannot possibly be given by any citizens.

18. It is therefore manifest, that in every city there is some one man, or council, or court, who by right hath as great a power over each single citizen, as each man hath over himself considered out of that civil state, that is, supreme and absolute,

to be limited only by the strength and forces of the city itself, and by nothing else in the world. For if his power were limited, that limitation must necessarily proceed from some greater power. For he that prescribes limits, must have a greater power than he who is confined by them. Now that confining power is either without limit, or is again restrained by some other greater than itself, and so we shall at length arrive to a power which hath no other limit, but that which is the *terminus ultimus* of the forces of all the citizens together. That same is called the supreme command; and if it be committed to a council, a supreme council, but if to one man, the supreme lord of the city. Now the notes of supreme command are these: to make and abrogate laws, to determine war and peace, to know and judge of all controversies, either by himself, or by judges appointed by him; to elect all magistrates, ministers, and counsellors. Lastly, if there be any man who by right can do some one action which is not lawful for any citizen or citizens to do beside himself, that man hath obtained the supreme power. For those things which by right may not be done by any one or many citizens, the city itself can only do. He therefore that doth those things useth the city's right, which is the supreme power.

19. They who compare a city and its citizens, with a man and his members, almost all say, that he who hath the supreme power in the city, is in relation to the whole city, such as the head is to the whole man. But it appears by what hath been already said, that he who is endued with such a power, (whether it be a man or a court) hath a relation to the city, not as that of the head, but of the soul to the body. For it is the soul by which a man hath a will, that is, can either will or nill; so by him who hath a will, that is, can either will or nill; so by him who hath the supreme power, and no otherwise, the city hath a will, and can either will or nill. A court of

counsellors is rather to be compared with the head, or one
counsellor, whose only counsel (if of any one alone) the chief
ruler makes use of in matters of greatest moment: for the
office of the head is to counsel, as the soul's is to command.

20. Forasmuch as the supreme command is constituted by
virtue of the compacts which each single citizen or subject
mutually makes with the other; but all contracts, as they receive their force from the contractors, so by their consent they
lose it again, and are broken; perhaps some may infer hence,
that by the consent of all the subjects together, the supreme
authority may be wholly taken away. Which inference, if it
were true, I cannot discern what danger would thence by right
arise to the supreme commanders. For since it is supposed that
each one hath obliged himself to each other, if any one of
them shall refuse, whatsoever the rest shall agree to do, he is
bound notwithstanding. Neither can any man without injury
to me, do that which by contract made with me, he hath
obliged himself not to do. But it is not to be imagined that
ever it will happen, that all the subjects together, not so much
as one excepted, will combine against the supreme power.
Wherefore there is no fear for rulers in chief, that by any
right they can be despoiled of their authority. If notwithstanding it were granted, that their right depended only on that
contract which each man makes with his fellow-citizen, it might
very easily happen, that they might be robbed of that dominion
under pretence of right; for subjects being called either by
the command of the city, or seditiously flocking together, most
men think that the consents of all are contained in the votes
of the greater part; which in truth is false. For it is not from
nature that the consent of the major part should be received
for the consent of all, neither is it true in tumults, but it proceeds from civil institution, and is then only true, when that
man or court which hath the supreme power, assembling his

subjects, by reason of the greatness of their number, allows those that are elected a power of speaking for those who elected them, and will have the major part of voices, in such matters as are by him propounded to be discussed, to be as effectual as the whole. But we cannot imagine that he who is chief, ever convened his subjects with intention that they should dispute his right, unless, weary of the burthen of his charge, he declared in plain terms, that he renounces and abandons his government. Now because most men through ignorance esteem not the consent of the major part of citizens only, but even of a very few, provided they be of their opinion, for the consent of the whole city, it may very well seem to them, that the supreme authority may by right be abrogated, so it be done in some great assembly of citizens by the votes of the greater number. But though a government be constituted by the contracts of particular men with particulars, yet its right depends not on that obligation only; there is another tie also towards him who commands. For each citizen compacting with his fellow, says thus: I convey my right on this party, upon condition that you pass yours to the same; by which means, that right which every man had before to use his faculties to his own advantage, is now wholly translated on some certain man or council for the common benefit. Wherefore what by the mutual contracts each one hath made with the other, what by the donation of right which every man is bound to ratify to him that commands, the government is upheld by a double obligation from the citizens, first, that which is due to their fellow-citizens, next, that which they owe to their prince. Wherefore no subjects, how many soever they be, can with any right despoil him who bears the chief rule, of his authority, even without his own consent.

Chapter VII

Of the Three Kinds of Government: Democracy, Aristocracy, Monarchy

1. We have already spoken of a city by institution in its genus; we will now say somewhat of its species. As for the difference of cities, it is taken from the difference of the persons, to whom the supreme power is committed. This power is committed either to one man, or council, or some one court consisting of many men. Furthermore, a council of many men consists either of all the citizens, (insomuch as every man of them hath a right to vote, and an interest in the ordering of the greatest affairs, if he will himself) or of a part only. From whence there arise three sorts of government; the one, when the power is in a council, where every citizen hath a right to vote; and it is called a democracy. The other, when it is in a council, where not all, but some part only have their suffrages; and we call it an aristocracy. The third is that, when the supreme authority rests only in one; and it is styled a monarchy. In the first, he that governs is called δῆμος, the people; in the second, the nobles; in the third, the monarch.

2. Now, although ancient writers of politics have introduced three other kinds of government opposite to these, to wit, anarchy or confusion to democracy, oligarchy, that is, the command of some few, to aristocracy, and tyranny to monarchy; yet are not these three distinct forms of government, but three diverse titles given by those who were either displeased with that present government, or those that bare rule. For men, by giving names, do usually, not only signify

the things themselves, but also their own affections, as love, hatred, anger, and the like. Whence it happens that what one man calls a democracy, another calls an anarchy; what one counts an aristocracy, another esteems an oligarchy; and whom one titles a king, another styles him a tyrant. So as we see, these names betoken not a diverse kind of government, but the diverse opinions of the subjects concerning him who hath the supreme power. For first, who sees not that anarchy is equally opposite to all the aforenamed forms? For that word signifies that there is no government at all, that is, not any city. But how is it possible that no city should be the species of a city? Furthermore, what difference is there between an oligarchy, which signifies the command of a few or grandees, or an aristocracy, which is that of the prime or chief heads, more than that men differ so among themselves, that the same things seem not good to all men? Whence it happens, that those persons, who by some are looked on as the best, are by others esteemed to be the worst of all men.

3. But men, by reason of their passions, will very hardly be persuaded that a kingdom and tyranny are not diverse kinds of cities; who though they would rather have the city subject to one than many, yet do they not believe it to be well governed unless it accord with their judgments. But we must discover by reason, and not by passion, what the difference is between a king and a tyrant. But first, they differ not in this, that a tyrant hath the greater power, for greater than the supreme cannot be granted; nor in this, that one hath a limited power, the other not; for he, whose authority is limited, is no king, but his subject that limits him. Lastly, neither differ they in their manner of acquisition; for if in a democratical or aristocratical government some one citizen should, by force, possess himself of the supreme power, if he gain the consent of all the citizens, he becomes a legitimate monarch; if not, he

is an enemy, not a tyrant. They differ therefore in the sole exercise of their command, insomuch as he is said to be a king, who governs well, and he a tyrant, that doth otherwise. The case therefore is brought to this pass, that a king, legitimately constituted in his government, if he seem to his subjects to rule well and to their liking, they afford him the appellation of a king; if not, they count him a tyrant. Wherefore we see a kingdom and tyranny are not diverse forms of government, but one and the self-same monarch hath the name of a king given him in point of honour and reverence to him, and of a tyrant in way of contumely and reproach. But what we frequently find in books said against tyrants, took its original from Greek and Roman writers, whose government was partly democratical, and partly aristocratical, and therefore not tyrants only, but even kings were odious to them.

4. There are, who indeed do think it necessary, that a supreme command should be somewhere extant in a city; but if it should be in any one, either man or council, it would follow (they say) that all the citizens must be slaves. Avoiding this condition, they imagine that there may be a certain form of government compounded of those three kinds we have spoken of, yet different from each particular, which they call a mixed monarchy, or mixed aristocracy, or mixed democracy, according as any one of these three sorts shall be more eminent than the rest. For example, if the naming of magistrates, and the arbitration of war and peace, should belong to the King, judicature to the Lords, and contribution of monies to the People, and the power of making laws to all together, this kind of state would they call a mixed monarchy forsooth. But if it were possible that there could be such a state, it would no whit advantage the liberty of the subject. For as long as they all agree, each single citizen is as much subject as possibly he can be: but if they disagree, the state returns to a civil war

and the right of the private sword, which certainly is much worse than any subjection whatsoever. But that there can be no such kind of government,* hath been sufficiently demonstrated in the foregoing chapter, art. 6-12.

5. Let us see a little now in the constituting of each form of government, what the constitutors do. Those who met together with intention to erect a city, were almost in the very act of meeting, a democracy. For in that they willingly met, they are supposed obliged to the observation of what shall be determined by the major part: which, while that convent lasts, or is adjourned to some certain days and places, is a clear democracy. For that convent, whose will is the will of all the citizens, hath the supreme authority; and because in this convent every man is supposed to have a right to give his voice, it follows that it is a democracy by the definition given in the first article of this chapter. But if they depart, and break up the convent, and appoint no time or place where and when they shall meet again, the public weal returns to anarchy and the same state it stood in before their meeting, that is, to the state of all men warring against all. The people, therefore, retains the supreme power no longer than there is a certain day and place publicly appointed and known, to which whosoever will

* Most men grant, that a government ought not to be divided, but they would have it moderated and bounded by some limits. Truly it is very reasonable it should be so; but if these men, when they speak of moderating and limiting, do understand dividing it, they make a very fond distinction. Truly, for my part, I wish that not only kings, but all other persons endued with supreme authority, would so temper themselves as to commit no wrong, and only minding their charges, contain themselves within the limits of the natural and divine laws. But they who distinguish thus, they would have the chief power bounded and restrained by others; which, because it cannot be done, but that they who do set the limits, must needs have some part of the power, whereby they may be enabled to do it, the government is properly divided, not moderated.

may resort. For except that be known and determined, they may either meet at divers times and places, that is, in factions, or not at all; and then it is no longer δῆμος, the people, but a dissolute multitude, to whom we can neither attribute any action or right. Two things therefore frame a democracy, whereof one (to wit, the perpetual prescription of convents) makes δῆμον, the people, the other (which is a plurality of voices) τὸ κράτος or the power.

6. Furthermore, it will not be sufficient for the people, so as to maintain its supremacy, to have some certain known times and places of meeting, unless that either the intervals of the times be of less distance, than that anything may in the meantime happen whereby (by reason of the defect of power) the city may be brought into some danger, or at least that the exercise of the supreme authority be, during the interval, granted to some one man or council. For unless this be done, there is not that wary care and heed taken for the defence and peace of single men, which ought to be, and therefore will not deserve the name of a city, because that in it, for want of security, every man's right of defending himself at his own pleasure returns to him again.

7. Democracy is not framed by contract of particular persons with the people, but by mutual compacts of single men each with other. But hence it appears, in the first place, that the persons contracting must be in being before the contract itself. But the people is not in being before the constitution of government, as not being any person, but a multitude of single persons; wherefore there could then no contract pass between the people and the subject. Now, if after that government is framed, the subject make any contract with the people, it is in vain; because the people contains within its will, the will of that subject to whom it is supposed to be obliged; and therefore may at its own will and pleasure dis-

engage itself, and by consequence is now actually free. But in the second place, that single persons do contract each with other may be inferred from hence, that in vain sure would the city have been constituted, if the citizens had been engaged by no contracts to do or omit what the city should command to be done or omitted. Because therefore such kind of compacts must be understood to pass as necessary to the making up of a city, but none can be made (as is already shewed) between the subject and the people; it follows, that they must be made between single citizens, namely, that each man contract to submit his will to the will of the major part, on condition that the rest also do the like. As if every one should say thus: I give up my right unto the people for your sake, on condition, that you also deliver up yours, for mine.

8. An aristocracy or council of nobles endowed with supreme authority, receives its original from a democracy, which gives up its right unto it, where we must understand that certain men distinguished from others, either by eminence of title, blood, or some other character, are propounded to the people, and by plurality of voices are elected, and being elected, the whole right of the people or city is conveyed on them, insomuch as whatsoever the people might do before, the same by right may this court of elected nobles now do. Which being done, it is clear that the people, considered as one person, (its supreme authority being already transferred on these) is no longer now in being.

9. As in democracy the people, so in an aristocracy the court of nobles is free from all manner of obligation; for seeing subjects not contracting with the people, but by mutual compacts among themselves, were tied to all that the people did; hence also they were tied to that act of the people in resigning up its right of government into the hands of nobles. Neither could this court, although elected by the people, be by it obliged

to anything. For being elected, the people is at once dissolved, as was declared above, and the authority it had as being a person utterly vanisheth. Wherefore the obligation which was due to the person must also vanish, and perish together with it.

10. Aristocracy hath these considerations, together with democracy. First, that without an appointment of some certain times and places, at which the court of nobles may meet, it is no longer a court, or one person, but a dissolute multitude without any supreme power. Secondly, that the times of their assembling cannot be disjoined by long intervals, without prejudice to the supreme power, unless its administration be transferred to some one man. Now the reasons why this happens, are the same which we set down in the fifth article.

11. As an aristocracy, so also a monarchy is derived from the power of the people, transferring its right, that is, its authority on one man. Here also we must understand, that some one man, either by name, or some other token, is propounded to be taken notice of above all the rest, and that by a plurality of voices the whole right of the people is conveyed on him, insomuch as whatsoever the people could do before he were elected, the same in every respect may he by right now do, being elected. Which being done, the people is no longer one person, but a rude multitude, as being only one before by virtue of the supreme command, whereof they now have made a conveyance from themselves on this one man.

12. And therefore neither doth the monarch oblige himself to any for the command he receives, for he receives it from the people; but as hath been shewed above, the people, as soon as that act is done, ceaseth to be a person; but the person vanishing, all obligation to the person vanisheth. The subjects therefore are tied to perform obedience to the monarch, by those compacts only by which they mutually obliged themselves to

the observation of all that the people should command them, that is, to obey that monarch, if he were made by the people.

13. But a monarchy differs as well from an aristocracy, as a democracy, in this chiefly, that in those there must be certain set times and places for deliberation and consultation of affairs, that is, for the actual exercise of it in all times and places. For the people or the nobles, not being one natural person, must necessarily have their meetings. The monarch, who is one by nature, is always in a present capacity to execute his authority.

14. Because we have declared above (in art. 7, 9, 12) that they who have gotten the supreme command are by no compacts obliged to any man, it necessarily follows, that they can do no injury to the subjects. For injury, according to the definition made in chap. III. art. 3, is nothing else but a breach of contract; and therefore where no contracts have part, there can be no injury. Yet the people, the nobles, and the monarch may diverse ways transgress against the other laws of nature, as by cruelty, iniquity, contumely, and other like vices, which come not under this strict and exact notion of injury. But if the subject yield not obedience to the supreme, he will in propriety of speech be said to be injurious, as well to his fellow-subjects, because each man hath compacted with the other to obey, as to his chief ruler, in resuming that right, which he hath given him, without his consent. And in a democracy or aristocracy, if anything be decreed against any law of nature, the city itself, that is, the civil person sins not, but those subjects only by whose votes it was decreed; for sin is a consequence of the natural express will, not of the political, which is artificial. For if it were otherwise, they would be guilty by whom the decree was absolutely disliked. But in a monarchy, if the monarch make any decree against the laws of nature, he sins himself, because in him the civil will and the natural are all one.

15. The people who are about to make a monarch, may give him the supremacy either simply without limitation of time, or for a certain season and time determined. If simply, we must understand that he who receives it, hath the self-same power which they had who gave it. On the same grounds, therefore, that the people by right could make him a monarch, may he make another monarch. Insomuch as the monarch to whom the command is simply given, receives a right not of possession only, but of succession also, so as he may declare whom he pleaseth for his successor.

16. But if the power be given for a time limited, we must have regard to somewhat more than the bare gift only. First, whether the people conveying its authority, left itself any right to meet at certain times and places, or not. Next, if it have reserved this power, whether it were done so as they might meet before that time were expired, which they pre-scribed to the monarch. Thirdly, whether they were contented to meet only at the will of that temporary monarch, and not otherwise. Suppose now the people had delivered up its power to some one man for term of life only; which being done, let us suppose in the first place, that every man departed from the council without making any order at all concerning the place, where (after his death) they should meet again to make a new election. In this case it is manifest by the fifth article of this chapter, that the people ceaseth to be a person, and is become a dissolute multitude, every one whereof hath an equal, to wit, a natural right to meet with whom he lists at divers times, and in what places shall best please him; nay, and if he can, engross the supreme power to himself, and settle it on his own head. What monarch soever, therefore, hath a command in such a condition, he is bound by the law of nature (set down in the article of the third chapter, of not returning evil for good) prudently to provide, that by his death the city suffer

not a dissolution, either by appointing a certain day and place, in which those subjects of his who have a mind to it may assemble themselves, or else by nominating a successor: whether of these shall to him seem most conducible to their common benefit. He therefore who on this aforesaid manner hath received his command during life, hath an absolute power, and may at his discretion dispose of the succession. In the next place, if we grant that the people departed not from the election of the temporary monarch, before they decreed a certain time and place of meeting after his death, then the monarch being dead, the authority is confirmed in the people, not by any new acts of the subjects, but by virtue of the former right. For all the supreme command (as dominion) was in the people, but the use and exercise of it was only in the temporary monarch, as in one that takes the benefit, but hath not the right. But if the people after the election of a temporary monarch, depart not from the court before they have appointed certain times and places to convene, during the time prescribed him (as the dictators in ancient times were made by the people of Rome), such an one is not to be accounted a monarch, but the prime officer of the people. And if it shall seem good, the people may deprive him of his office even before that time, as the people of Rome did, when they conferred an equal power on Minutius, master of the horse, with Quintus Fabius Maximus, whom before they had made dictator. The reason whereof is, that it is not to be imagined, that he, whether man or council, who hath the readiest and most immediate power to act, should hold his command on such terms, as not to be able actually to execute it; for command is nothing else but a right of commanding, as oft as nature allows it possible. Lastly, if the people having declared a temporary monarch, depart from the court on such terms, as it shall not be lawful for them to meet without the command of the monarch, we must under-

stand the people to be immediately dissolved, and that his
authority who is thus declared, is absolute; forasmuch as it is
not in the power of all the subjects to frame the city anew,
unless he give consent who hath now alone the authority. Nor
matters it, that he hath perhaps made any promise to assemble
his subjects on some certain times; since there remains no person now in being, but at his discretion, to whom the promise
was made. What we have spoken of these four cases of a
people electing a temporary monarch will be more clearly explained by comparing them with an absolute monarch, who
hath no heir-apparent. For the people is lord of the subject in
such a manner as there can be no heir but whom itself doth
appoint. Besides, the spaces between the times of the subjects' meeting may be fitly compared to those times wherein the
monarch sleeps; for in either, the acts of commanding cease,
the power remains. Furthermore, to dissolve the convent, so as
it cannot meet again, is the death of the people; just as
sleeping, so as he can never wake more, is the death of a
man. As therefore a king, who hath no heir, going to his rest,
so as never to rise again, that is, dying, if he commit the exercise of his regal authority to any one till he awake, does by
consequence give him the succession; the people also electing
a temporary monarch, and not reserving a power to convene,
delivers up to him the whole dominion of the country. Furthermore, as a king going to sleep for some season, entrusts the
administration of his kingdom to some other, and waking takes
it again; so the people having elected a temporary monarch,
and withal retaining a right to meet at a certain day and place,
at that day receives its supremacy again. And as a king who
hath committed the execution of his authority to another, himself in the meanwhile waking, can recall this commission
again when he pleaseth; so the people, who during the time
prescribed to the temporary monarch doth by right convene,

may if they please, deprive the monarch of his authority. Lastly, the king, who commits his authority to another while himself sleeps, not being able to wake again till he whom he entrusted give consent, loses at once both his power and his life; so the people, who hath given the supreme power to a temporary monarch in such sort as they cannot assemble without his command, is absolutely dissolved, and the power remains with him whom they have chosen.

17. If the monarch promise aught to any one, or many subjects together, by consequence whereof the exercise of his power may suffer prejudice, that promise or compact, whether made by oath or without it, is null. For all compact is a conveyance of right, which by what hath been said in the fourth article of the second chapter, requires meet and proper signs of the will in the conveyer. But he who sufficiently signifies his will of retaining the end, doth also sufficiently declare that he quits not his right to the means necessary to that end. Now he who hath promised to part with somewhat necessary to the supreme power, and yet retains the power itself, gives sufficient tokens, that he no otherwise promised it than so far forth as the power might be retained without it. Whensoever therefore it shall appear that what is promised cannot be performed without prejudice to the power, the promise must be valued as not made, that is, of no effect.

18. We have seen how subjects, nature dictating, have obliged themselves by mutual compacts to obey the supreme power. We will see now by what means it comes to pass that they are released from these bonds of obedience. And first of all, this happens by rejection, namely, if a man cast off or forsake, but convey not the right of his command on some other. For what is thus rejected, is openly exposed to all alike, catch who catch can; whence again, by the right of nature, every subject may heed the preservation of himself according to his own

judgment. In the second place, if the kingdom fall into the power of the enemy, so as there can no more opposition be made against them, we must understand that he, who before had the supreme authority, hath now lost it: for when the subjects have done their full endeavour to prevent their falling into the enemy's hands, they have fulfilled those contracts of obedience which they made each with other, and what, being conquered, they promise afterwards, to avoid death, they must, with no less endeavour, labour to perform. Thirdly, in a monarchy, (for a democracy and aristocracy cannot fail), if there be no successor, all the subjects are discharged from their obligations; for no man is supposed to be tied he knows not to whom, for in such a case it were impossible to perform aught. And by these three ways, all subjects are restored from their civil subjection to that liberty, which all men have to all things, to wit, natural and savage, (for the natural state hath the same proportion to the civil, I mean liberty to subjection, which passion hath to reason, or a beast to a man). Furthermore, each subject may lawfully be freed from his subjection by the will of him who hath the supreme power, namely, if he change his soil; which may be done two ways, either by permission, as he who gets license to dwell in another country, or command, as he who is banished. In both cases he is free from the laws of his former country, because he is tied to observe those of the latter.

Chapter VIII

Of the Rights of Lords Over Their Servants

1. In the two foregoing chapters we have treated of an institutive or framed government, as being that which receives its original from the consent of many, who by contract and faith mutually given have obliged each other. Now follows what may be said concerning a natural government; which may also be called acquired, because it is that which is gotten by power and natural force. But we must know in the first place by what means the right of dominion may be gotten over the persons of men. Where such a right is gotten, there is a kind of a little kingdom; for to be a king, is nothing else but to have dominion over many persons; and thus a great family is a kingdom, and a little kingdom a family. Let us return again to the state of nature, and consider men as if but even now sprung out of the earth, and suddenly (like mushrooms) come to full maturity, without all kind of engagement to each other. There are but three ways only, whereby one can have a dominion over the person of another; whereof the first is, if by mutual contract made between themselves (for peace and self-defence's sake) they have willingly given up themselves to the power and authority of some man, or council of men; and of this we have already spoken. The second is, if a man taken prisoner in the wars, or overcome, or else distrusting his own forces, (to avoid death) promises the conqueror or the stronger party his service, that is, to do all whatsoever he shall command him. In which contract, the good which the vanquished or inferior in strength doth receive, is the grant of his life, which

by the right of war in the natural state of men he might have been deprived of; but the good which he promises, is his service and obedience. By virtue therefore of this promise, there is as absolute service and obedience due from the vanquished to the vanquisher, as possibly can be, excepting what repugns the divine laws; for he who is obliged to obey the commands of any man before he knows what he will command him, is simply and without any restriction tied to the performance of all commands whatsoever. Now he that is thus tied, is called a servant; he to whom he is tied, a lord. Thirdly, there is a right acquired over the person of a man by generation; of which kind of acquisition somewhat shall be spoken in the following chapter.

2. Every one that is taken in the war, and hath his life spared him, is not supposed to have contracted with his lord; for every one is not trusted with so much of his natural liberty, as to be able, if he desired it, either to fly away, or quit his service, or contrive any mischief to his lord. And these serve indeed, but within prisons, or bound within irons; and therefore they were called not by the common name of servant only, but by the peculiar name of slave, even as now at this day, *un serviteur,* and *un serf,* or *un esclave* have diverse significations.

3. The obligation therefore of a servant to his lord ariseth not from a simple grant of his life, but from hence rather, that he keeps him not bound or imprisoned. For all obligation derives from contract; but where is no trust, there can be no contract, as appears by chap. ii. art. 9, where a compact is defined to be the promise of him who is trusted. There is therefore a confidence and trust which accompanies the benefit of pardoned life, whereby the lord affords him his corporal liberty; so that if no obligation nor bonds of contract had happened, he might not only have made his escape, but also have killed his lord, who was the preserver of his life.

4. Wherefore such kind of servants as are restrained by imprisonment or bonds, are not comprehended in that definition of servants given above, because those serve not for the contract's sake, but to the end they may not suffer. And therefore if they fly, or kill their lord, they offend not against the laws of nature. For to bind any man is a plain sign, that the binder supposes him that is bound, not to be sufficiently tied by any other obligation.

5. The lord therefore hath no less dominion over a servant that is not, than over one that is bound; for he hath a supreme power over both, and may say of his servant no less than of another thing, whether animate or inanimate, this is mine. Whence it follows, that whatsoever the servant had before his servitude, that afterwards becomes the lord's; and whatsoever he hath gotten, it was gotten for his lord. For he that can by right dispose of the person of a man, may surely dispose of all those things which that person could dispose of. There is therefore nothing which the servant may retain as his own against the will of his lord; yet hath he, by his lord's distribution, a propriety and dominion over his own goods, insomuch as one servant may keep and defend them against the invasion of his fellow-servant, in the same manner as hath been shewed before, that a subject hath nothing properly his own against the will of the supreme authority, but every subject hath a propriety against his fellow-subject.

6. Since therefore both the servant himself, and all that belongs to him are his lord's, and by the right of nature every man may dispose of his own in what manner he pleases; the lord may either sell, lay to pledge, or by testament convey the dominion he hath over his servant, according to his own will and pleasure.

7. Furthermore, what hath before been demonstrated concerning subjects in an institutive government, namely, that he

who hath the supreme power can do his subject no injury; is true also concerning servants, because they have subjected their will to the will of the Lord. Wherefore, whatsoever he doth, it is done with their wills, but no injury can be done to him that willeth it.

8. But if it happen that the lord, either by captivity or voluntary subjection, doth become a servant or subject to another, that other shall not only be lord of him, but also of his servants; supreme lord over these, immediate lord over him. Now because not the servant only, but also all he hath, are his lord's; therefore his servants now belong to this man, neither can the mediate lord dispose otherwise of them than shall seem good to the supreme. And therefore, if sometime in civil governments the lord have an absolute power over his servants, that is supposed to be derived from the right of nature, and not constituted, but slightly passed over by the civil law.

9. A servant is by the same manner freed from his servitude, that a subject in an institutive government is freed from his subjection. First, if his lord enfranchise him; for the right which the servant transferred to his lord over himself, the same may the lord restore to the servant again. And this manner of bestowing of liberty is called manumission; which is just as if a city should permit a citizen to convey himself under the jurisdiction of some other city. Secondly, if the lord cast off his servant from him, which in a city is banishment; neither differs it from manumission in effect, but in manner only. For there, liberty is granted as a favour, here, as a punishment: in both. the dominion is renounced. Thirdly, if the servant be taken prisoner, the old servitude is abolished by the new; for as all other things, so servants also are acquired by war, whom in equity the lord must protect, if he will have them to be his. Fourthly, the servant is freed for want of knowledge of a successor, the lord dying (suppose) without

any testament or heir. For no man is understood to be obliged,
unless he know to whom he is to perform the obligation.
Lastly, the servant that is put in bonds, or by any other means
deprived of his corporal liberty, is freed from that other obligation of contract. For there can be no contract where there is
no trust, nor can that faith be broken which is not given. But
the lord who himself serves another, cannot so free his servants,
but that they must still continue under the power of the supreme; for, as hath been shewed before, such servants are not
his, but the supreme lord's.

10. We get a right over irrational creatures in the same
manner, that we do over the persons of men, to wit, by force
and natural strength. For if in the state of nature it is lawful
for every one, by reason of that war which is of all against
all, to subdue and also to kill men as oft as it shall seem to
conduce unto their good, much more will the same be lawful
against brutes; namely, at their own discretion, to reduce those
to servitude which by art may be tamed and fitted for use,
and to persecute and destroy the rest by a perpetual war, as
dangerous and noxious. Our dominion therefore over beasts,
hath its original from the right of nature, not from divine
positive right. For if such a right had not been before the publishing of the Sacred Scriptures, no man by right might have
killed a beast for his food, but he to whom the divine pleasure
was made manifest by holy writ; a most hard condition for
men indeed whom the beasts might devour without injury,
and yet they might not destroy them. Forasmuch therefore as it
proceeds from the right of nature, that a beast may kill a man,
it is also by the same right, that a man may slay a beast.

CHAPTER IX

OF THE RIGHT OF PARENTS OVER THEIR CHILDREN, AND OF HEREDITARY GOVERNMENT

1. SOCRATES *is a man, and therefore a living creature,* is right reasoning, and that most evident, because there is nothing needful to the acknowledging of the truth of the consequence, but that the word man be understood, because a living creature is in the definition itself of a man, and every one makes up the proposition which was desired, namely this, man is a living creature. And this, *Sophroniscus is Socrates' father, and therefore his lord,* is perhaps a true inference, but not evident, because the word lord is not in the definition of a father: wherefore it is necessary, to make it more evident, that the connexion of father and lord be somewhat unfolded. Those that have hitherto endeavoured to prove the dominion of a parent over his children, have brought no other argument than that of generation, as if it were of itself evident, that what is begotten by me is mine; just as if a man should think, that because there is a triangle, it appears presently without any further discourse, that its angles are equal to two right. Besides, since dominion, that is, supreme power is indivisible, insomuch as no man can serve two masters, but two persons, male and female, must concur in the act of generation; it is impossible that dominion should at all be acquired by generation only. Wherefore we will, with the more diligence, in this place inquire into the original of paternal government.

2. We must therefore return to the state of nature, in which, by reason of the equality of nature, all men of riper years are

to be accounted equal. There by right of nature the conqueror is lord of the conquered. By the right therefore of nature, the dominion over the infant first belongs to him who first hath him in his power. But it is manifest that he who is newly born, is in the mother's power before any others, insomuch as she may rightly, and at her own will, either breed him up, or adventure him to fortune.

3. If therefore she breed him (because the state of nature is the state of war) she is supposed to bring him up on this condition, that being grown to full age he become not her enemy; which is, that he obey her. For since by natural necessity we all desire that which appears good unto us, it cannot be understood that any man hath on such terms afforded life to another, that he might both get strength by his years, and at once become an enemy. But each man is an enemy to that other whom he neither obeys nor commands. And thus in the state of nature, every woman that bears children, becomes both a mother and a lord. But what some say, that in this case the father, by reason of the pre-eminence of sex, and not the mother, becomes lord, signifies nothing. For both reason shows the contrary, because the inequality of their natural forces is not so great, that the man could get the dominion over the woman without war, and custom also contradicts not. For women, namely Amazons, have in former times waged war against their adversaries, and disposed of their children at their own wills. And at this day in divers places, women are invested with the principal authority. Neither do their husbands dispose of their children, but themselves; which in truth they do by the right of nature; forasmuch as they who have the supreme power, are not tied at all (as hath been shewed) to the civil laws. Add also that in the state of nature it cannot be known who is the father, but by the testimony of the mother; the child therefore is his whose the mother will have it, and therefore hers. Where-

fore original dominion over children belongs to the mother: and among men no less than other creatures, the birth follows the belly.

4. The dominion passes from the mother to others, divers ways. First, if she quit and forsake her right by exposing the child. He therefore that shall bring up the child thus exposed, shall have the same dominion over it which the mother had. For that life which the mother had given it (not by getting, but nourishing it), she now by exposing takes from it; wherefore the obligation also which arose from the benefit of life, is by this exposition made void. Now the preserved oweth all to the preserver, whether in regard of his education as to a mother, or of his service as to a lord. For although the mother in the state of nature, where all men have a right to all things, may recover her son again (namely, by the same right that anybody else might do it), yet may not the son rightly transfer himself again unto his mother.

5. Secondly, if the mother be taken prisoner, her son is his that took her, because that he who hath dominion over the person, hath also dominion over all belonging to the person; wherefore over the son also, as hath been shewed in the foregoing chapter, in the fifth article. Thirdly, if the mother be a subject under what government soever, he that hath the supreme authority in that government, will also have the dominion over him that is born of her; for he is lord also of the mother, who is bound to obey him in all things. Fourthly, if a woman for society's sake give herself to a man on this condition, that he shall bear the sway, he that receives his being from the contribution of both parties, is the father's in regard of the command he hath over the mother. But if a woman bearing rule shall have children by a subject, the children are the mother's; for otherwise the woman can have no children without prejudice to her authority. And universally, if the society of

the male and female be such an union, as the one have subjected himself to the other, the children belong to him or her that commands.

6. But in the state of nature, if a man and woman contract so, as neither is subject to the command of the other, the children are the mother's, for the reasons above given in the third article, unless by pacts it be otherwise provided. For the mother may by pact dispose of her right as she lists, as heretofore hath been done by the Amazons, who of those children which have been begotten by their neighbours, have by pact allowed them the males, and retained the females to themselves. But in a civil government, if there be a contract of marriage between a man and woman, the children are the father's, because in all cities, to wit, constituted of fathers, not mothers governing their families, the domestical command belongs to the man; and such a contract, if it be made according to the civil laws, is called matrimony. But if they agree only to lie together, the children are the father's or the mother's variously, according to the differing civil laws of divers cities.

7. Now because, by the third article, the mother is originally lord of her children, and from her the father, or somebody else by derived right, it is manifest that the children are no less subject to those by whom they are nourished and brought up, than servants to their lords, and subjects to him who bears the supreme rule; and that a parent cannot be injurious to his son, as long as he is under his power. A son also is freed from subjection in the same manner as a subject and servant are. For emancipation is the same thing with manumission, and abdication with banishment.

8. The enfranchised son or released servant, do now stand in less fear of their lord and father, being deprived of his natural and lordly power over them, and (if regard be had to true and inward honour) do honour him less than before. For

honour (as hath been said in the section above) is nothing else but the estimation of another's power; and therefore he that hath least power, hath always least honour. But it is not to be imagined that the enfranchiser ever intended so to match the enfranchised with himself, as that he should not so much as acknowledge a benefit, but should so carry himself in all things, as if he were become wholly his equal. It must therefore be ever understood, that he who is freed from subjection, whether he be a servant, son, or some colony, doth promise all those external signs at least, whereby superiors used to be honoured by their inferiors. From whence it follows, that the precept of honouring our parents, belongs to the law of nature, not only under the title of gratitude, but also of agreement.

9. What then, will some one demand, is the difference between a son, or between a subject and a servant? Neither do I know that any writer hath fully declared what liberty, and what slavery is. Commonly to do all things according to our own fancies, and that without punishment, is esteemed to be liberty; not to be able to do this, is judged bondage; which in a civil government, and with the peace of mankind, cannot possibly be done, because there is no city without a command and a restraining right. Liberty, that we may define it, is nothing else but an absence of the lets and hindrances of motion; as water shut up in a vessel is therefore not at liberty, because the vessel hinders it from running out; which, the vessel being broken, is made free. And every man hath more or less liberty, as he hath more or less space in which he employs himself: as he hath more liberty, who is in a large, than he that is kept in a close prison. And a man may be free toward one part, and yet not toward another, as the traveller is bounded on this and that side with hedges or stone walls, lest he spoil the vines or corn, neighbouring on the highway. And these kinds of lets are external and absolute. In which

sense all servants and subjects are free, who are not fettered and imprisoned. There are others which are arbitrary, which do not absolutely hinder motion, but by accident, to wit, by our own choice; as he that is in a ship is not so hindered, but he may cast himself into the sea, if he will. And here also the more ways a man may move himself, the more liberty he hath. And herein consists civil liberty; for no man, whether subject, son, or servant, is so hindered by the punishments appointed by the city, the father, or the lord, how cruel soever, but that he may do all things, and make use of all means necessary to the preservation of his life and health. For my part therefore I cannot find what reason a mere servant hath to make complaints, if they relate only to want of liberty, unless he count it a misery to be restrained from hurting himself, and to receive that life, (which by war, or misfortune, or through his own idleness was forfeited) together with all manner of sustenance, and all things necessary to the conservation of health, on this condition only, that he will be ruled. For he that is kept in by punishments laid before him, so as he dares not let loose the reins to his will in all things, is not oppressed by servitude, but is governed and sustained. But this privilege free subjects and sons of a family have above servants (in every government and family where servants are): that they may both undergo the more honourable offices of the city or family, and also enjoy a larger possession of things superfluous. And herein lies the difference between a free subject and a servant, that he is free indeed, who serves his city only; but a servant is he who also serves his fellow-subject. All other liberty is an exemption from the laws of the city, and proper only to those that bear rule.

10. A father, with his sons and servants, grown into a civil person by virtue of his paternal jurisdiction, is called a family. This family, if through multiplying of children and acquisition of servants it becomes numerous, insomuch as without casting

the uncertain die of war it cannot be subdued, will be termed an hereditary kingdom; which though it differ from an institutive monarchy, being acquired by force, in the original and manner of its constitution; yet being constituted, it hath all the same properties, and the right of authority is everywhere the same, insomuch as it is not needful to speak anything of them apart.

11. It hath been spoken, by what right supreme authorities are constituted. We must now briefly tell you by what right they may be continued. Now the right by which they are continued, is that which is called the right of succession. Now because in a democracy, the supreme authority is with the people, as long as there be any subjects in being, so long it rests with the same person; for the people hath no successor. In like manner in an aristocracy, one of the nobles dying, some other by the rest is substituted in his place; and therefore except they all die together, which I suppose will never happen, there is no succession. The query therefore of the right of succession takes place only in an absolute monarchy. For they who exercise the supreme power for a time only, are themselves no monarchs, but ministers of state.

12. But first, if a monarch shall by testament appoint one to succeed him, the person appointed shall succeed. For if he be appointed by the people, he shall have all the right over the city which the people had, as hath been showed in chap. VII. art. 11. But the people might choose him; by the same right therefore may he choose another. But in an hereditary kingdom, there are the same rights as in an institutive. Wherefore, every monarch may by his will make a successor.

13. But what a man may transfer on another by testament, that by the same right may he, yet living, give or sell away. To whomsoever therefore he shall make over the supreme power, whether by gift or sale, it is rightly made.

14. But if living he have not declared his will concerning his successor by testament nor otherwise, it is supposed, first, that he would not have his government reduced to an anarchy or the state of war, that is, to the destruction of his subjects; as well because he could not do that without breach of the laws of nature, whereby he was obliged to the performance of all things necessarily conducing to the preservation of peace, as also because, if that had been his will, it had not been hard for him to have declared that openly. Next, because the right passeth according to the will of the father, we must judge of the successor according to the signs of his will. It is understood therefore, that he would have his subjects to be under a monarchical government, rather than any other, because he himself in ruling hath before approved of that state by his example, and hath not afterward either by any word or deed condemned it.

15. Furthermore, because by natural necessity all men wish them better, from whom they receive glory and honour, than others; but every man after death receives honour and glory from his children, sooner than from the power of any other men: hence we gather, that a father intends better for his children, than any other person's. It is to be understood therefore, that the will of the father, dying without testament, was that some of his children should succeed him. Yet this is to be understood with this proviso, that there be no more apparent tokens to the contrary: of which kind, after many successions, custom may be one. For he that makes no mention of his succession, is supposed to consent to the customs of his realm.

16. Among children the males carry the pre-eminence; in the beginning perhaps, because for the most part (although not always) they are fitter for the administration of greater matters, but specially of wars; but afterwards, when it was grown a custom, because that custom was not contradicted.

And therefore the will of the father, unless some other custom or sign do clearly repugn it, is to be interpreted in favour of them.

17. Now because the sons are equal, and the power cannot be divided, the eldest shall succeed. For if there be any difference by reason of age, the eldest is supposed more worthy; for nature being judge, the most in years (because usually it is so) is the wisest. But other judge there cannot be had. But if the brothers must be equally valued, the succession shall be by lot. But primogeniture is a natural lot, and by this the eldest is already preferred; nor is there any that hath power to judge, whether by this or any other kind of lots the matter is to be decided. Now the same reason which contends thus for the first-born son, doth no less for the first-born daughter.

18. But if he have no children, then the command shall pass to his brothers and sisters, for the same reason, that the children should have succeeded if he had had them. For those that are nearest to us in nature, are supposed to be nearest in benevolence; and to his brothers sooner than his sisters, and to the elder sooner than the younger; for the reason is the same for these that it was for the children.

19. Furthermore, by the same reason that men succeed to the power, do they also succeed to the right of succession. For if the first-born die before the father, it will be judged, that he transferred his right of succession unto his children, unless the father have otherwise decreed it. And therefore the nephews will have a fairer pretence to the succession, than the uncles. I say all these things will be thus, if the custom of the place (which the father by not contradicting will be judged to have consented to) do not hinder them.

Chapter X

Comparison Between Three Kinds of Government, According to Their Several Inconveniences

1. WHAT democracy, aristocracy, and monarchy are, hath already been spoken; but which of them tends most to the preservation of the subjects' peace, and procuring their advantages, we must see by comparing them together. But first let us set forth the advantages and disadvantages of a city in general, lest some perhaps should think it better, that every man be left to live at his own will, than to constitute any civil society at all. Every man indeed out of the state of civil government hath a most entire, but unfruitful liberty; because that he who by reason of his own liberty acts all at his own will, must also by reason of the same liberty in others suffer all at another's will. But in a constituted city, every subject retains to himself as much freedom as suffices him to live well and quietly, and there is so much taken away from others, as may make them not to be feared. Out of this state, every man hath such a right to all, as yet he can enjoy nothing; in it, each one securely enjoys his limited right. Out of it, any man may rightly spoil or kill another; in it, none but one. Out of it, we are protected by our own forces; in it, by the power of all. Out of it, no man is sure of the fruit of his labours; in it, all men are. Lastly, out of it, there is a dominion of passions, war, fear, poverty, slovenliness, solitude, barbarism, ignorance, cruelty; in it, the dominion of reason, peace, security, riches, decency, society, elegancy, sciences, and benevolence.

2. Aristotle, in his seventh book and fourteenth chapter of

his *Politics,* saith, that there are two sorts of governments, whereof the one relates to the benefit of the ruler, the other to that of the subjects; as if where subjects are severely dealt with, there were one, and where more mildly, there were another form of government. Which opinion may by no means be subscribed to; for all the profits and disprofits arising from government are the same, and common both to the ruler and the subject. The damages which befall some particular subjects through misfortune, folly, negligence, sloth, or his own luxury, may very well be severed from those which concern the ruler. But those relate not to the government itself, being such as may happen in any form of government whatsoever. If these same happen from the first institution of the city, they will then be truly called the inconveniences of government; but they will be common to the ruler with his subjects, as their benefits are common. But the first and greatest benefit, peace and defence, is to both; for both he that commands, and he who is commanded, to the end that he may defend his life, makes use at once of all the forces of his fellow-subjects. And in the greatest inconvenience that can befall a city, namely, the slaughter of subjects, arising from anarchy, both the commander, and the parties commanded, are equally concerned. Next, if the ruler levy such a sum of vast moneys from his subjects, as they are not able to maintain themselves and their families, nor conserve their bodily strength and vigor, the disadvantage is as much his as theirs, who, with never so great a stock or measure of riches, is not able to keep his authority or his riches without the bodies of his subjects. But if he raise no more than is sufficient for the due administration of his power, that is a benefit equal to himself and his subjects, tending to a common peace and defence. Nor is it imaginable which way public treasures can be a grievance to private subjects, if they be not so exhausted, as to be wholly deprived from all possibility to acquire,

even by their industry, necessaries to sustain the strength of
their bodies and minds. For even thus the grievance would concern the ruler; nor would it arise from the ill-institution or
ordination of the government, (because in all manner of governments subjects may be oppressed) but from the ill administration of a well established government.

3. Now that monarchy, of the foresaid forms, of democracy,
aristocracy, and monarchy, hath the pre-eminence, will best
appear by comparing the conveniences and inconveniences arising in each one of them. Those arguments therefore, that the
whole universe is governed by one God; that the ancients preferred the monarchical state before all others, ascribing the rule
of the gods to one Jupiter; that in the beginning of affairs and
of nations, the decrees of princes were held for laws; that
paternal government, instituted by God himself in the creation,
was monarchical; that other governments were compacted by
the artifice of men * out of the ashes of monarchy, after it had
been ruined with seditions; and that the people of God were
under the jurisdiction of kings: although, I say, these do hold
forth monarchy as the more eminent to us, yet because they do
it by examples and testimonies, and not by solid reason, we
will pass them over.

4. Some there are who are discontented with the government under one, for no other reason, but because it is under

---

* It seems the ancients who made that same fable of Prometheus
pointed at this. They say that Prometheus, having stolen fire from the
sun, formed a man out of clay, and that for this deed he was tortured
by Jupiter with a perpetual gnawing in his liver, which is, that by human
invention (which is signified by Prometheus) laws and justice were by
imitation taken from monarchy; by virtue whereof (as by fire removed
from its natural orb) the multitude (as the dirt and dregs of men) was
as it were quickened and formed into a civil person; which is termed
aristocracy or democracy. But the author and abettors being found, who
might securely and quietly have lived under the natural jurisdiction of
kings, do thus smart for it; that being exposed still to alteration, they
are tormented with perpetual cares, suspicions, and dissensions.

one; as if it were an unreasonable thing, that one man among so many should so far excel in power, as to be able at his own pleasure to dispose of all the rest. These men, sure, if they could, would withdraw themselves from under the dominion of one God. But this exception against one is suggested by envy, while they see one man in possession of what all desire. For the same cause they would judge it to be as unreasonable, if a few commanded, unless they themselves either were, or hoped to be of the number. For if it be an unreasonable thing that all men have not an equal right, surely an aristocracy must be unreasonable also. But because we have showed that the state of equality is the state of war, and that therefore inequality was introduced by a general consent; this inequality whereby he, whom we have voluntarily given more to, enjoys more, is no longer to be accounted an unreasonable thing. The inconveniences therefore which attend the dominion of one man, attend his person, not his unity. Let us therefore see whether brings with it the greater grievances to the subject, the command of one man, or of many.

5. But first, we must remove their opinion who deny that to be any city at all, which is compacted of never so great a number of servants under a common lord. In the ninth article of the fifth chapter, a city is defined to be one person made out of many men, whose will by their own contracts is to be esteemed as the wills of them all, insomuch as he may use the strength and faculties of each single person for the public peace and safety. And by the same article of the same chapter, one person is that, when the wills of many are contained in the will of one. But the will of each servant is contained in the will of his lord, as hath been declared in the fifth article of the eighth chapter, so as he may employ all their forces and faculties according to his own will and pleasure. It follows therefore that that must needs be a city, which is constituted

by a lord and many servants. Neither can any reason be brought
to contradict this which doth not equally combat against a city
constituted by a father and his sons. For to a lord who hath
no children, servants are in the nature of sons; for they are
both his honour and safeguard; neither are servants more subject to their lords, than children to their parents, as hath been
manifested above in the fifth article of the eighth chapter.

6. Among other grievances of supreme authority one is, that
the ruler, beside those monies necessary for public charges, as
the maintaining of public ministers, building, and defending
of castles, waging wars, honourably sustaining his own household, may also, if he will, exact others through his lust, whereby
to enrich his sons, kindred, favourites, and flatterers too. I
confess this is a grievance, but of the number of those which
accompany all kinds of government, but are more tolerable in
a monarchy than in a democracy. For though the monarch
would enrich them, they cannot be many, because belonging but
to one. But in a democracy, look how many demagogues, that
is, how many powerful orators there are with the people (which
ever are many, and daily new ones growing), so many children,
kinsmen, friends, and flatterers are to be rewarded. For every
of them desire not only to make their families as potent, as
illustrious in wealth, as may be, but also to oblige others to
them by benefits for the better strengthening of themselves.
A monarch may in great part satisfy his officers and friends,
because they are not many, without any cost to his subjects,
I mean, without robbing them of any of those treasures given
in for the maintenance of war and peace. In a democracy,
where many are to be satisfied, and always new ones, this cannot be done without the subjects' oppression. Though a monarch may promote unworthy persons, yet oft times he will not
do it; but in a democracy all the popular men are therefore
supposed to do it, because it is necessary; for else the power

of them who did it would so increase, as it would not only become dreadful to those others, but even to the whole city also.

7. Another grievance is, that same perpetual fear of death which every man must necessarily be in, while he considers with himself that the ruler hath power not only to appoint what punishments he lists on any transgressions, but that he may also in his wrath and sensuality slaughter his innocent subjects, and those who never offended against the laws. And truly this is a very great grievance in any form of government, wheresoever it happens; for it is therefore a grievance, because it is, not because it may be done. But it is the fault of the ruler, not of the government. For all the acts of Nero are not essential to monarchy; yet subjects are less often undeservedly condemned under one ruler, than under the people. For kings are only severe against those who either trouble them with impertinent counsels, or oppose them with reproachful words, or control their wills; but they are the cause that that excess of power which one subject might have above another becomes harmless. Wherefore some Nero or Caligula reigning, no men can undeservedly suffer, but such as are known to him, namely, courtiers, and such as are remarkable for some eminent charge, and not all neither, but they only who are possessed of what he desires to enjoy. For they that are offensive, and contumelious, are deservedly punished. Whosoever therefore in a monarchy will lead a retired life, let him be what he will that reigns, he is out of danger. For the ambitious only suffer; the rest are protected from the injuries of the more potent. But in a popular dominion, there may be as many Neros as there are orators who soothe the people. For each one of them can do as much as the people, and they mutually give way to each other's appetite (as it were by this secret pact, spare me to-day and I'll spare thee to-morrow) while they exempt those from punishment, who, to satisfy their lust and private hatred, have unde-

servedly slain their fellow-subjects. Furthermore, there is a certain limit in private power, which if it exceed, it may prove pernicious to the realm, and by reason whereof it is necessary sometimes for monarchs to have a care that the common weal do thence receive no prejudice. When therefore this power consisted in the multitude of riches, they lessened it by diminishing their heaps; but if it were in popular applause, the powerful party, without any other crime laid to his charge, was taken from among them. The same was usually practised in democracies. For the Athenians inflicted a punishment of ten years' banishment on those that were powerful, merely because of their powers, without the guilt of any other crime. And those who by liberal gifts did seek the favour of the common people, were put to death at Rome, as men ambitious of a kingdom. In this democracy and monarchy were even; yet differed they much in fame, because fame derives from the people, and what is done by many, is commended by many. And therefore what the monarch does, is said to be done out of envy to their virtues, which if it were done by the people, would be accounted policy.

8. There are some who therefore imagine monarchy to be more grievous than democracy, because there is less liberty in that, than in this. If by liberty they mean an exemption from, that subjection which is due to the laws, that is, the commands of the people, neither in democracy, nor in any other state of government whatsoever, is there any such kind of liberty. If they suppose liberty to consist in this, that there be few laws, few prohibitions, and those too such, that except they were forbidden, there could be no peace; then I deny that there is more liberty in democracy than monarchy; for the one as truly consisteth with such a liberty, as the other. For although the word liberty may in large and ample letters be written over the gates of any city whatsoever, yet is it not meant the subject's,

but the city's liberty; neither can that word with better right be inscribed on a city which is governed by the people, than that which is ruled by a monarch. But when private men or subjects demand liberty, under the name of liberty they ask not for liberty, but dominion, which yet for want of understanding they little consider. For if every man would grant the same liberty to another, which he desires for himself, as is commanded by the law of nature, that same natural state would return again, in which all men may by right do all things; which if they knew, they would abhor, as being worse than all kinds of civil subjection whatsoever. But if any man desire to have his single freedom, the rest being bound, what does he else demand but to have the dominion? For whoso is freed from all bonds, is lord over all those that still continue bound. Subjects therefore have no greater liberty in a popular, than in a monarchical state. That which deceives them, is the equal participation of command and public places. For where the authority is in the people, single subjects do so far forth share in it as they are parts of the people ruling; and they equally partake in public offices so far forth as they have equal voices in choosing magistrates and public ministers. And this is that which Aristotle aimed at, himself also, through the custom of that time, miscalling dominion liberty (*Politics,* Book vi, Chapter 2): In a popular state there is liberty by supposition; which is a speech of the vulgar, as if no man were free out of this state. From whence, by the way, we may collect, that those subjects who in a monarchy deplore their lost liberty, do only stomach this, that they are not received to the steerage of the commonweal.

9. But perhaps for this very reason some will say, that a popular state is much to be preferred before a monarchical; because that, where all men have a hand in public businesses, there all have an opportunity to shew their wisdom, knowledge,

and eloquence, in deliberating matters of the greatest difficulty and moment, which by reason of that desire of praise which is bred in human nature, is to them who excel in such-like faculties, and seem to themselves to exceed others, the most delightful of all things. But in a monarchy, this same way to obtain praise and honour, is shut up to the greatest part of subjects; and what is a grievance, if this be none? I will tell you: to see his opinion, whom we scorn, preferred before ours; to have our wisdom undervalued before our own faces; by an uncertain trial of a little vain glory, to undergo most certain enmities (for this cannot be avoided, whether we have the better or the worse); to hate, and to be hated, by reason of the disagreement of opinions; to lay open our secret councils and advices to all, to no purpose, and without any benefit; to neglect the affairs of our own family: these, I say, are grievances. But to be absent from a trial of wits, although those trials are pleasant to the eloquent, is not therefore a grievance to them, unless we will say, that it is a grievance to valiant men to be restrained from fighting, because they delight in it.

10. Besides, there are many reasons why deliberations are less successful in great assemblies, than in lesser councils. Whereof one is, that to advise rightly of all things conducing to the preservation of a commonweal, we must not only understand matters at home, but foreign affairs too; at home, by what goods the country is nourished and defended, and whence they are fetched; what places are fit to make garrisons of; by what means soldiers are best to be raised and maintained; what manner of affections the subjects bear towards their prince or governors of their country; and many the like; abroad, what the power of each neighbouring country is, and wherein it consists; what advantage or disadvantage we may receive from them; what their dispositions are both to us-ward, and how affected to each other among themselves; and what counsel

daily passeth among them. Now, because very few in a great assembly of men understand these things, being for the most part unskilful (that I say not incapable) of them, what can that same number of advisers with their impertinent opinions contribute to good counsels, other than mere lets and impediments?

11. Another reason why a great assembly is not so fit for consultation is, because every one who delivers his opinion holds it necessary to make a long-continued speech; and to gain the more esteem from his auditors, he polishes and adorns it with the best and smoothest language. Now the nature of eloquence is to make good and evil, profitable and unprofitable, honest and dishonest, appear to be more or less than indeed they are; and to make that seem just which is unjust, according as it shall best suit with his end that speaketh. For this is to persuade; and though they reason, yet take they not their rise from true principles, but from vulgar received opinions, which, for the most part, are erroneous; neither endeavour they so much to fit their speech to the nature of the things they speak of, as to the passions of their minds to whom they speak, whence it happens that opinions are delivered not by right reason, but by a certain violence of mind. Nor is this fault in the man, but in the nature itself of eloquence, whose end (as all the masters of rhetoric teach us) is not truth (except by chance) but victory, and whose property is not to inform, but to allure.

12. The third reason why men advise less successfully in a great convent is, because that thence arise factions in a commonweal, and out of factions, seditions and civil war. For when equal orators do combat with contrary opinions and speeches, the conquered hates the conqueror and all those that were of his side, as holding his council and wisdom in scorn, and studies all means to make the advice of his adversaries preju-

dicial to the state; for thus he hopes to see the glory taken from him, and restored unto himself. Furthermore, where the votes are not so unequal, but that the conquered have hopes, by the accession of some few of their own opinion, at another sitting to make the stronger party, the chief heads do call the rest together; they advise a part how they may abrogate the former judgment given; they appoint to be the first and earliest at the next convent; they determine what, and in what order, each man shall speak, that the same business may again be brought to agitation; that so what was confirmed before by the number of their then present adversaries, the same may now in some measure become of no effect to them, being negligently absent. And this same kind of industry and diligence which they use to make a people, is commonly called a faction. But when a faction is inferior in votes, and superior, or not much inferior in power, then what they cannot obtain by craft and language, they attempt by force of arms; and so it comes to a civil war. But some will say, these things do not necessarily, nor often happen. He may as well say, that the chief parties are not necessarily desirous of vain glory, and that the greatest of them seldom disagree in great matters.

13. It follows hence, that when the legislative power resides in such convents as these, the laws must needs be inconstant, and change, not according to the alteration of the state of affairs, nor according to the changeableness of men's minds, but as the major part, now of this, then of that faction, do convene; insomuch as the laws do float here and there, as it were upon the waters.

14. In the fourth place, the counsels of great assemblies have this inconvenience, that whereas it is oft of great consequence that they should be kept secret, they are for the most part discovered to the enemy before they can be brought to any effect,

and their power and will is as soon known abroad, as to the people itself commanding at home.

15. These inconveniences which are found in the deliberations of great assemblies do so far forth evince monarchy to be better than democracy, as in democracy affairs of great consequence are oftener trusted to be discussed by such like committees, than in a monarchy. Neither can it easily be done otherwise. For there is no reason why every man should not naturally mind his own private, than the public business, but that here he sees a means to declare his eloquence, whereby he may gain the reputation of being ingenious and wise, and returning home to his friends, to his parents, to his wife and children, rejoice and triumph in the applause of his dexterous behaviour. As of old, all the delight Marcus Coriolanus had in his warlike actions, was to see his praises so well pleasing to his mother. But if the people in a democracy would bestow the power of deliberating in matters of war and peace, either on one, or some very few, being content with the nomination of magistrates and public ministers, that is to say, with the authority without the ministration, then it must be confessed, that in this particular democracy and monarchy would be equal.

16. Neither do the conveniences or inconveniences which are found to be more in one kind of government than another, arise from hence, namely, because the government itself, or the administration of its affairs, are better committed to one, than many; or on the other side, to many, than to some few. For government is the power, the administration of it is the act. Now the power in all kinds of government is equal; the acts only differ, that is to say, the actions and motions of a commonweal, as they flow from the deliberations of many or few, of skilful or impertinent men. Whence we understand, that the conveniences or inconveniences of any government depend not on him in whom the authority resides, but on his officers;

and therefore nothing hinders, but that the commonweal may be well governed, although the monarch be a woman, or youth, or infant, provided that they be fit for affairs, who are endued with the public offices and charges. And that which is said, *woe to the land whose king is a child,* doth not signify the condition of a monarchy to be inferior to a popular state, but contrariwise, that by accident it is the grievance of a kingdom, that the king being a child, it often happens, that many by ambition and power intruding themselves into public councils, the government comes to be administered in a democratical manner, and that thence arise those infelicities which for the most part accompany the dominion of the people.

17. But it is a manifest sign, that the most absolute monarchy is the best state of government, that not only kings, but even those cities which are subject to the people or to nobles, give the whole command of war to one only, and that so absolute, as nothing can be more (wherein by the way this must be noted also, that no king can give a general greater authority over his army, than he himself by right may exercise over all his subjects). Monarchy therefore is the best of all governments in the camps. But what else are many commonwealths, than so many camps strengthened with arms and men against each other, whose state (because not restrained by any common power, howsoever an uncertain peace, like a short truce, may pass between them) is to be accounted for the state of nature, which is the state of war.

18. Lastly, since it was necessary for the preservation of ourselves to be subject to some man or council, we cannot on better condition be subject to any, than one whose interest depends upon our safety and welfare; and this then comes to pass when we are the inheritance of the ruler. For every man of his own accord endeavours the preservation of his inheritance. But the lands and monies of the subjects are not only

the prince's treasure, but their bodies and wildy minds; which
will be easily granted by those who consider at how great rates
the dominion of lesser countries is valued, and how much easier
it is for men to procure money, than money men. Nor do we
readily meet with any example that shows us when any subject, without any default of his own, hath by his prince been
despoiled of his life or goods, through the sole licentiousness
of his authority.

19. Hitherto we have compared a monarchical with a popular state; we have said nothing of aristocracy. We may conclude of this, by what hath been said of those, that that which
is hereditary, and content with the election of magistrates;
which transmits its deliberations to some few, and those most
able; which simply imitates the government of monarchs most,
and the people least of all; is for the subjects both better and
more lasting than the rest.

Chapter XI

Places and Examples of Scripture of the
Rights of Government

(The text of this chapter is omitted.)

CHAPTER XII

OF THE INTERNAL CAUSES TENDING TO THE DISSOLUTION
OF ANY GOVERNMENT

1. HITHERTO hath been spoken by what causes and pacts commonweals are constituted, and what the rights of princes are over their subjects. Now we will briefly say somewhat concerning the causes which dissolve them, or the reasons of seditions. Now as in the motion of natural bodies three things are to be considered, namely, internal disposition, that they be susceptible of the motion to be produced; the external agent, whereby a certain and determined motion may in act be produced; and the action itself: so also in a commonweal where the subjects begin to raise tumults, three things present themselves to our regard; first, the doctrines and the passions contrary to peace, wherewith the minds of men are fitted and disposed; next, their quality and condition who solicit, assemble, and direct them, already thus disposed, to take up arms and quit their allegiance; lastly, the manner how this is done, or the faction itself. But one and the first which disposeth them to sedition, is this, that the knowledge of good and evil belongs to each single man. In the state of nature indeed, where every man lives by equal right, and has not by any mutual pacts submitted to the command of others, we have granted this to be true, in chap. i. art. 9. But we have also shown that in a civil state the laws were the rules of good and evil, just and unjust, honest and dishonest; that therefore what the legislator commands, must be held for good, and what he forbids for evil; and the legislator is ever that person

who hath the supreme power in the commonweal, that is to say, the monarch in a monarchy. We have confirmed the same truth in chap. XI. art. 2, out of the words of Solomon. For if private men may pursue that as good, and shun that as evil, which appears to them to be so, to what end serve those words of his: *Give therefore unto thy servant an understanding heart to judge thy people, that I may discern between good and evil?* Since therefore it belongs to kings to discern between good and evil, wicked are those, though usual, sayings, that he only is a king who does righteously, and that kings must not be obeyed, unless they command us just things, and many other such like. Before there was any government, just and unjust had no being, their nature only being relative to some command, and every action in its own nature is indifferent; that it becomes just or unjust, proceeds from the right of the magistrate. Legitimate kings therefore make the things they command just, by commanding them, and those which they forbid, unjust, by forbidding them. But private men, while they assume to themselves the knowledge of good and evil, desire to be even as kings, which cannot be with the safety of the commonweal. The most ancient of all God's commands is, (Gen. ii. 17): *Thou shalt not eat of the tree of knowledge of good and evil;* and the most ancient of all diabolical temptations, (Gen. iii. 5): *Ye shall be as gods, knowing good and evil;* and God's first expostulation with man, (verse 11): *Who told thee that thou wert naked? Hast thou eaten of the tree, whereof I commanded thee that thou shouldst not eat?* As if he had said, how comest thou to judge that nakedness, wherein it seemed good to me to create thee, to be shameful, except thou have arrogated to thyself the knowledge of good and evil?

2. Whatsoever any man doth against his conscience is a sin; for he who doth so, contemns the law. But we must distinguish. That is my sin indeed, which committing I do believe to be

my sin; but what I believe to be another man's sin, I may sometimes do that without any sin of mine. For if I be commanded to do that which is a sin in him who commands me, if I do it, and he that commands me be by right lord over me, I sin not. For if I wage war at the commandment of my prince, conceiving the war to be unjustly undertaken, I do not therefore do unjustly, but rather if I refuse to do it, arrogating to myself the knowledge of what is just and unjust, which pertains only to my prince. They who observe not this distinction, will fall into a necessity of sinning, as oft as anything is commanded them, which either is, or seems to be unlawful to them: for if they obey, they sin against their conscience, and if they obey not, against right. If they sin against their conscience, they declare that they fear not the pains of the world to come; if they sin against right, they do, as much as in them lies, abolish human society and the civil life of the present world. Their opinion therefore who teach, that subjects sin when they obey their prince's commands which to them seem unjust, is both erroneous, and to be reckoned among those which are contrary to civil obedience; and it depends upon that original error which we have observed above, in the foregoing article. For by our taking upon us to judge of good and evil, we are the occasion, that as well our obedience, as disobedience, becomes sin unto us.

3. The third seditious doctrine springs from the same root, that tyrannicide is lawful; nay, at this day it is by many divines, and of old it was by all the philosophers, Plato, Aristotle, Cicero, Seneca, Plutarch, and the rest of the maintainers of the Greek and Roman anarchies, held not only lawful, but even worthy of the greatest praise. And under the title of tyrants, they mean not only monarchs, but all those who bear the chief rule in any government whatsoever; for not Pisistratus only at Athens, but those Thirty also who succeeded him, and ruled

together, were all called tyrants. But he, whom men require to be put to death as being a tyrant, commands either by right or without right; if without right, he is an enemy, and by right to be put to death; but then this must not be called the killing a tyrant, but an enemy; if by right, then the divine interrogation takes place: Who hath told thee that he was a tyrant? Hast thou eaten of the tree whereof I commanded thee that thou shouldst not eat? For why dost thou call him a tyrant, whom God hath made a king, except that thou, being a private person, usurpest to thyself the knowledge of good and evil? But how pernicious this opinion is to all governments, but especially to that which is monarchical, we may hence discern, namely, that by it every king, whether good or ill, stands exposed to be condemned by the judgment, and slain by the hand of every murderous villain.

4. The fourth opinion adversary to civil society, is theirs who hold, that they who bear rule are subject also to the civil laws. Which hath been sufficiently proved before not to be true, in chap. vi. art. 14, from this argument: that a city can neither be bound to itself, nor to any subject; not to itself, because no man can be obliged except it be to another; not to any subject, because the single wills of the subjects are contained in the will of the city, insomuch that if the city will be free from all such obligation, the subjects will so too; and by consequence she is so. But that which holds true in a city, that must be supposed to be true in a man, or an assembly of men, who have the supreme authority; for they make a city, which hath no being but by their supreme power. Now that this opinion cannot consist with the very being of government, is evident from hence, that by it the knowledge of what is good and evil, that is to say, the definition of what is, and what is not against the laws, would return to each single person. Obedience therefore will cease as oft as anything seems to be commanded contrary

to the civil laws, and together with it, all coercive jurisdiction, which cannot possibly be without the destruction of the very essence of government. Yet this error hath great props, Aristotle and others; who, by reason of human infirmity, suppose the supreme power to be committed with most security to the laws only. But they seem to have looked very shallowly into the nature of government, who thought that the constraining power, the interpretation of laws, and the making of laws, (all which are powers necessarily belonging to government) should be left wholly to the laws themselves. Now although particular subjects may sometimes contend in judgment, and go to law with the supreme magistrate; yet this is only then, when the question is not what the magistrate may, but what by a certain rule he hath declared he would do. As, when by any law the judges sit upon the life of a subject, the question is not whether the magistrate could by his absolute right deprive him of his life; but whether by that law his will was that he should be deprived of it. But his will was, he should, if he brake the law; else, his will was, he should not. This therefore, that a subject may have an action of law against his supreme magistrate, is not strength of argument sufficient to prove, that he is tied to his own laws. On the contrary, it is evident, that he is not tied to his own laws, because no man is bound to himself. Laws therefore are set for Titius and Caius, not for the ruler. However, by the ambition of lawyers, it is so ordered, that the laws to unskilful men seem not to depend on the authority of the magistrate, but their prudence.

5. In the fifth place, that the supreme authority may be divided, is a most fatal opinion to all commonweals. But diverse men divide it diverse ways. For some divide it so as to grant a supremacy to the civil power in matters pertaining to peace and the benefits of this life, but in things concerning the salvation of the soul they transfer it on others. Now, be-

cause justice is of all things most necessary to salvation, it happens that subjects measuring justice, not as they ought, by the civil laws, but by the precepts and doctrines of them who, in regard of the magistrate, are either private men or strangers, through a superstitious fear dare not perform the obedience due to their princes, through fear falling into that which they most feared. Now what can be more pernicious to any state, than that men should, by the apprehension of everlasting torments, be deterred from obeying their princes, that is to say, the laws; or from being just? There are also some who divide the supreme authority so as to allow the power of war and peace unto one (whom they call a monarch) but the right of raising money they give to some others, and not to him. But because monies are the sinews of war and peace, they who thus divide the authority, do either really not divide it at all, but place it wholly in them, in whose power the money is, but give the name of it to another, or if they do really divide it, they dissolve the government. For neither upon necessity can war be waged, nor can the public peace be preserved without money.

6. It is a common doctrine, that faith and holiness are not acquired by study, and natural reason, but are always supernaturally infused, and inspired into men. Which, if it were true, I understand not why we should be commanded to give an account of our faith; or why any man, who is truly a Christian, should not be a prophet; or lastly, why every man should not judge what is fit for him to do, what to avoid, rather out of his own inspiration, than by the precepts of his superiors or right reason. A return therefore must be made to the private knowledge of good and evil; which cannot be granted without the ruin of all governments. This opinion hath spread itself so largely through the whole Christian world, that the number of apostates from natural reason is almost become infinite. And it sprang from sick-brained men, who having gotten good store

of holy words by frequent reading of the Scriptures, made such a connexion of them usually in their preaching, that their sermons, signifying just nothing, yet to unlearned men seemed most divine; for he whose nonsense appears to be a divine speech, must necessarily seem to be inspired from above.

7. The seventh doctrine opposite to government, is this, that each subject hath an absolute dominion over the goods he is in possession of, that is to say, such a propriety as excludes not only the right of all the rest of his fellow-subjects to the same goods, but also of the magistrate himself. Which is not true; for they who have a lord over them, have themselves no lordship, as hath been proved, chap. viii. art. 5. Now the magistrate is lord of all his subjects, by the constitution of government. Before the yoke of civil society was undertaken, no man had any proper right; all things were common to all men. Tell me therefore, how gottest thou this propriety but from the magistrate? How got the magistrate it, but that every man transferred his right on him? And thou therefore hast also given up, thy right to him. Thy dominion therefore, and propriety, is just so much as he will, and shall last so long as he pleases; even as in a family, each son hath such proper goods, and so long lasting, as seems good to the father. But the greatest part of men who profess civil prudence, reason otherwise; we are equal (say they) by nature; there is no reason why any man should by better right take my goods from me, than I his from him; we know that money sometimes is needful for the defence and maintenance of the public; but let them, who require it, show us the present necessity, and they shall willingly receive it. They who talk thus know not, that what they would have, is already done from the beginning, in the very constitution of government, and therefore speaking as in a dissolute multitude and yet not fashioned government, they destroy the frame.

8. In the last place, it is a great hindrance to civil government, especially monarchical, that man distinguish not enough between a people and a multitude. The people is somewhat that is one, having one will, and to whom one action may be attributed; none of these can properly be said of a multitude. The people rules in all governments. For even in monarchies the people commands; for the people wills by the will of one man; but the multitude are citizens, that is to say, subjects. In a democracy and aristocracy, the citizens are the multitude, but the court is the people. And in a monarchy, the subjects are the multitude, and (however it seem a paradox) the king is the people. The common sort of men, and others who little consider these truths, do always speak of a great number of men as of the people, that is to say, the city; they say that the city hath rebelled against the king (which is impossible), and that the people will, and nill, what murmuring and discontented subjects would have, or would not have, under pretence of the people stirring up the citizens against the city, that is to say, the multitude against the people. And these are almost all the opinions wherewith subjects being tainted do easily tumult. And forasmuch as in all manner of government majesty is to be preserved by him or them who have the supreme authority, the *crimen læsæ majestatis* naturally cleaves to these opinions.

9. There is nothing more afflicts the mind of man than poverty, or the want of those things which are necessary for the preservation of life and honour. And though there be no man but knows, that riches are gotten with industry, and kept by frugality, yet all the poor commonly lay the blame on the evil government, excusing their own sloth and luxury, as if their private goods forsooth were wasted by public exactions. But men must consider, that they who have no patrimony, must not only labour that they may live, but fight too, that they may labour. Every one of the Jews, who in Esdras' time built

the walls of Jerusalem, did the work with one hand, and held the sword in the other. In all government we must conceive that the hand which holds the sword is the king or supreme council, which is no less to be sustained and nourished by the subjects' care and industry, than that wherewith each man procures himself a private fortune; and that customs and tributes are nothing else but their reward who watch in arms for us, that the labours and endeavours of single men may not be molested by the incursion of enemies; and that their complaint, who impute their poverty to public persons, is not more just, than if they should say that they are become in want by paying of their debts. But the most part of men consider nothing of these things. For they suffer the same thing with them who have a disease they call an incubus; which springing from gluttony, it makes men believe they are invaded, oppressed, and stifled with a great weight. Now it is a thing manifest of itself, that they who seem to themselves to be burthened with the whole load of the commonweal, are prone to be seditious; and that they are affected with change, who are distasted at the present state of things.

10. Another noxious disease of the mind is theirs, who having little employment, want honour and dignity. All men naturally strive for honour and preferment; but chiefly they who are least troubled with caring for necessary things. For these men are invited by their vacancy, sometimes to disputation among themselves concerning the commonweal, sometimes to an easy reading of histories, politics, orations, poems, and other pleasant books; and it happens that hence they think themselves sufficiently furnished both with wit and learning, to administer matters of the greatest consequence. Now because all men are not what they appear to themselves, and if they were, yet all (by reason of the multitude) could not be received to public offices, it is necessary that many must be passed by.

These therefore conceiving themselves affronted, can desire nothing more, partly out of envy to those who were preferred before them, partly out of hope to overwhelm them, than ill-success to the public consultations. And therefore it is no marvel if with greedy appetites they seek for occasions of innovations.

11. The hope of overcoming is also to be numbered among other seditious inclinations. For let there be as many men as you will, infected with opinions repugnant to peace and civil government; let there be as many as there can, never so much wounded and torn with affronts and calumnies by them who are in authority; yet if there be no hope of having the better of them, or it appear not sufficient, there will no sedition follow; every man will dissemble his thoughts, and rather content himself with the present burthen, than hazard a heavier weight. There are four things necessarily requisite to this hope: numbers, instruments, mutual trust, and commanders. To resist public magistrates without a great number, is not sedition, but desperation. By instruments of war I mean all manner of arms, munition, and other necessary provision, without which, number can do nothing; nor arms neither, without mutual trust; nor all these, without union under some commander, whom of their own accord they are content to obey; not as being engaged by their submission to his command (for we have already in this very chapter, supposed these kind of men not to understand, being obliged beyond that which seems right and good in their own eyes) but for some opinion they have of his virtue, or military skill, or resemblance of humours. If these four be near at hand to men grieved with the present state, and measuring the justice of their actions by their own judgments, there will be nothing wanting to sedition and confusion of the realm, but one to stir up and quicken them.

12. Sallust's character of Cataline (than whom there never was a greater artist in raising seditions) is this: that he had

great eloquence, and little wisdom. He separates wisdom from eloquence, attributing this as necessary to a man born for commotions, adjudging that as an instructress of peace and quietness. Now eloquence is twofold. The one is an elegant and clear expression of the conceptions of the mind, and riseth partly from the contemplation of the things themselves, partly from an understanding of words taken in their own proper and definite signification. The other is a commotion of the passions of the mind (such as are hope, fear, anger, pity) and derives from a metaphorical use of words fitted to the passions. That forms a speech from true principles; this from opinions already received, what nature soever they are of. The art of that is logic, of this rhetoric; the end of that is truth, of this victory. Each hath its use; that in deliberations, this in exhortations; for that is never disjoined from wisdom, but this almost ever. But that this kind of powerful eloquence, separated from the true knowledge of things, that is to say, from wisdom, is the true character of them who solicit and stir up the people to innovations, may easily be gathered out of the work itself which they have to do. For they could not poison the people with those absurd opinions contrary to peace and civil society, unless they held them themselves, which sure is an ignorance greater than can well befall any wise man. For he that knows not whence the laws derive their power, which are the rules of just and unjust, honest and dishonest, good and evil; what makes and preserves peace among men, what destroys it; what is his, and what another's; lastly, what he would have done to himself (that he may do the like to others): is surely to be accounted but meanly wise. But that they can turn their auditors out of fools into madmen; that they can make things to them who are ill-affected seem worse, to them who are well-affected seem evil; that they can enlarge their hopes, lessen their dangers beyond reason: this they have from that sort of eloquence, not which explains things as they are, but from that other, which by moving their minds, makes all things to appear to be such as they in their minds prepared before, had already conceived them.

13. Many men, who are themselves very well affected to civil society, do through want of knowledge co-operate to the disposing of subjects' minds to sedition, whilst they teach young men a doctrine conformable to the said opinions in their schools, and all the people in their pulpits. Now they who desire to bring this disposition into act, place their whole endeavour in this: first, that they may join the ill-affected together into faction and conspiracy; next, that themselves may have the greatest stroke in the faction. They gather them into faction, while they make themselves the relators and interpreters of the counsels and actions of single men, and nominate the persons and places, to assemble and deliberate of such things whereby the present government may be reformed, according as it shall seem best to their interests. Now to the end that they themselves may have the chief rule in the faction, the faction must be kept in a faction, that is to say, they must have their secret meetings apart with a few, where they may order what shall afterward be propounded in a general meeting, and by whom, and on what subject, and in what order each of them shall speak, and how they may draw the powerfullest and most popular men of the faction to their side. And thus when they have gotten a faction big enough, in which they may rule by their eloquence, they move it to take upon it the managing of affairs, and thus they sometimes oppress the commonwealth, namely, where there is no other faction to oppose them; but for the most part they rend it, and introduce a civil war. For folly and eloquence concur in the subversion of government, in the same manner (as the fable hath it) as heretofore the daughters of Pelias, king of

Thessaly, conspired with Medea against their father. They
going to restore the decrepit old man to his youth again by
the counsel of Medea, they cut him into pieces, and set him in
the fire to boil, in vain expecting when he would live again.
So the common people, through their folly (like the daughters
of Pelias) desiring to renew the ancient government, being
drawn away by the eloquence of ambitious men, as it were
by the witchcraft of Medea, divided into faction, they consume
it rather by those flames, than they reform it.

Chapter XIII

Concerning the Duties of Them Who Bear Rule

1. By what hath hitherto been said, the duties of citizens and subjects in any kind of government whatsoever, and the power of the supreme ruler over them are apparent. But we have as yet said nothing of the duties of rulers, and how they ought to behave themselves towards their subjects. We must then distinguish between the right and the exercise of supreme authority, for they can be divided; as for example, when he who hath the right, either cannot or will not be present in judging trespasses, or deliberating of affairs. For kings sometimes by reason of their age cannot order their affairs, sometimes also, though they can do it themselves, yet they judge it fitter, being satisfied in the choice of their officers and counsellors, to exercise their power by them. Now where the right and exercise are severed, there the government of the commonweal is like the ordinary government of the world, in which God, the mover of all things, produceth natural effects by the means of secondary causes. But where he, to whom the right of ruling doth belong, is himself present in all judicatures, consultations, and public actions, there the administration is such, as if God, beyond the ordinary course of nature, should immediately apply himself unto all matters. We will therefore in this chapter summarily and briefly speak somewhat concerning their duties who exercise authority, whether by their own or other's right. Nor is it my purpose to descend into those things, which being diverse

from others, some princes may do, for this is to be left to
the political practices of each commonweal.

2. Now all the duties of rulers are contained in this one
sentence, the safety of the people is the supreme law. For
although they who among men obtain the chiefest dominion,
cannot be subject to laws properly so called, that is to say, to
the will of men, because to be chief, and subject, are contradictories; yet is it their duty in all things, as much as possibly
they can, to yield obedience unto right reason, which is the
natural, moral, and divine law. But because dominions were
constituted for peace's sake, and peace was sought after for
safety's sake, he, who being placed in authority, shall use his
power otherwise than to the safety of the people, will act
against the reasons of peace, that is to say, against the laws of
nature. Now as the safety of the people dictates a law by which
princes know their duty, so doth it also teach them an art
how to procure themselves a benefit; for the power of the
citizens is the power of the city, that is to say, his that bears
the chief rule in any state.

3. By the people in this place we understand, not one civil
person, namely, the city itself which governs, but the multitude of subjects which are governed. For the city was not
instituted for its own, but for the subjects' sake; and yet a
particular care is not required of this or that man. For the
ruler (as such) provides no otherwise for the safety of his people, than by his laws, which are universal; and therefore he
hath fully discharged himself, if he have thoroughly endeavoured by wholesome constitutions, to establish the welfare of
the most part, and made it as lasting as may be; and that no
man suffer ill, but by his own default, or by some chance
which could not be prevented. But it sometimes conduces to
the safety of the most part, that wicked men do suffer.

4. But by safety must be understood, not the sole preserva-

tion of life in what condition soever, but in order to its happiness. For to this end did men freely assemble themselves, and institute a government, that they might, as much as their human condition would afford, live delightfully. They therefore who had undertaken the administration of power in such a kind of government, would sin against the law of nature (because against their trust who had committed that power unto them), if they should not study, as much as by good laws could be effected, to furnish their subjects abundantly, not only with the good things belonging to life, but also with those which advance to delectation. They who have acquired dominion by arms, do all desire that their subjects may be strong in body and mind, that they may serve them the better. Wherefore if they should not endeavour to provide them, not only with such things whereby they may live, but also with such whereby they may grow strong and lusty, they would act against their own scope and end.

5. And first of all, princes do believe that it mainly concerns eternal salvation, what opinions are held of the Deity, and what manner of worship he is to be adored with. Which being supposed, it may be demanded whether chief rulers, and whosoever they be, whether one or more, who exercise supreme authority, sin not against the law of nature, if they cause not such a doctrine and worship to be taught and practised (or permit a contrary to be taught and practised) as they believe necessarily conduceth to the eternal salvation of their subjects. It is manifest that they act against their conscience, and that they will, as much as in them lies, the eternal perdition of their subjects; for if they willed it not, I see no reason why they should suffer (when being supreme they cannot be compelled) such things to be taught and done, for which they believe them to be in a damnable state. But we will leave this difficulty in suspense.

6. The benefits of subjects respecting this life only, may be distributed into four kinds. 1. That they be defended against foreign enemies. 2. That peace be preserved at home. 3. That they be enriched as much as may consist with public security. 4. That they enjoy a harmless liberty. For supreme commanders can confer no more to their civil happiness, than that being preserved from foreign and civil wars, they may quietly enjoy that wealth which they have purchased by their own industry.

7. There are two things necessary for the people's defence; to be warned and to be forearmed. For the state of commonwealths considered in themselves, is natural, that is to say, hostile. Neither if they cease from fighting, is it therefore to be called peace, but rather a breathing time, in which one enemy observing the motion and countenance of the other, values his security not according to the pacts, but the forces and counsels of his adversary. And this by natural right, as hath been showed in chap. II. art. 11, from this, that contracts are invalid in the state of nature, as oft as any just fear doth intervene. It is therefore necessary to the defence of the city, first, that there be some who may, as near as may be, search into and discover the counsels and motions of all those who may prejudice it. For discoverers to ministers of state, are like the beams of the sun to the human soul. And we may more truly say in vision political, than natural, that the sensible and intelligible species of outward things, not well considered by others, are by the air transported to the soul (that is to say, to them who have the supreme authority) and therefore are they no less necessary to the preservation of the state, than the rays of the light are to the conservation of man. Or if they be compared to spider's webs, which, extended on all sides by the finest threads, do warn them, keeping in their small holes, of all outward motions. They who bear rule can no

more know what is necessary to be commanded for the defence of their subjects without spies, than those spiders can, when they shall go forth, and whether they shall repair, without the motion of those threads.

8. Furthermore, it is necessarily requisite to the people's defence, that they be forearmed. Now to be forearmed is to be furnished with soldiers, arms, ships, forts, and monies, before the danger be instant; for the listing of soldiers and taking up of arms after a blow is given, is too late at least, if not impossible. In like manner, not to raise forts and appoint garrisons in convenient places, before the frontiers are invaded, is to be like those country swains (as Demosthenes said) who, ignorant of the art of fencing, with their bucklers guarded those parts of the body where they first felt the smart of the strokes. But they who think it then seasonable enough to raise monies for the maintenance of soldiers and other charges of war, when the danger begins to show itself, they consider not surely how difficult a matter it is to wring suddenly out of close-fisted men so vast a proportion of monies. For almost all men, what they once reckon in the number of their goods, do judge themselves to have such a right and propriety in it, as they conceive themselves to be injured whensoever they are forced to employ but the least part of it for the public good. Now a sufficient stock of monies to defend the country with arms, will not soon be raised out of the treasure of imposts and customs. We must therefore, for fear of war, in time of peace hoard up good sums, if we intend the safety of the commonweal. Since therefore it necessarily belongs to rulers, for the subjects' safety, to discover the enemy's counsel, to keep garrisons, and to have money in continual readiness, and that princes are, by the law of nature, bound to use their whole endeavour in procuring the welfare of their subjects, it follows, that it is not only lawful for them to send out spies, to main-

tain soldiers, to build forts, and to require monies for these purposes, but also, not to do thus, is unlawful. To which also may be added, whatsoever shall seem to conduce to the lessening of the power of foreigners whom they suspect, whether by slight or force. For rulers are bound according to their power to prevent the evils they suspect, lest peradventure they may happen through their negligence.

9. But many things are required to the conservation of inward peace, because many things concur (as hath been showed in the foregoing chapter) to its perturbation. We have there showed, that some things there are which dispose the minds of men to sedition, others which move and quicken them so disposed. Among those which dispose them, we have reckoned in the first place certain perverse doctrines. It is therefore the duty of those who have the chief authority, to root those out of the minds of men, not by commanding, but by teaching; not by the terror of penalties, but by the perspicuity of reasons. The laws whereby this evil may be withstood are not to be made against the persons erring, but against the errors themselves. Those errors which, in the foregoing chapter, we affirmed were inconsistent with the quiet of the commonweal, have crept into the minds of ignorant men, partly from the pulpit, partly from the daily discourses of men, who, by reason of little employment, otherwise do find leisure enough to study; and they got into these men's minds by the teachers of their youth in public schools. Wherefore also, on the other side, if any man would introduce sound doctrine, he must begin from the academies. There the true and truly demonstrated foundations of civil doctrine are to be laid, wherewith young men being once endued, they may afterward, both in private and public, instruct the vulgar. And this they will do so much the more cheerfully and powerfully, by how much themselves shall be more certainly convinced of the truth of those things

they profess and teach. For seeing at this day men receive propositions, though false, and no more intelligible than if a man should join together a company of terms drawn by chance out of an urn, by reason of the frequent use of hearing them; how much more would they for the same reason entertain true doctrines, suitable to their own understandings and the nature of things? I therefore conceive it to be the duty of supreme officers to cause the true elements of civil doctrine to be written, and to command them to be taught in all the colleges of their several dominions.

10. In the next place we showed that grief of mind arising from want did dispose the subjects to sedition, which want, although derived from their own luxury and sloth, yet they impute it to those who govern the realm, as though they were drained and oppressed by public pensions. Notwithstanding, it may sometimes happen that this complaint may be just, namely, when the burthens of the realm are unequally imposed on the subjects; for that which to all together is but a light weight, if many withdraw themselves, it will be very heavy, nay, even intolerable to the rest: neither are men wont so much to grieve at the burthen itself, as at the inequality. With much earnestness therefore men strive to be freed from taxes; and in this conflict the less happy, as being overcome, do envy the more fortunate. To remove therefore all just complaint, it is the interest of the public quiet, and by consequence it concerns the duty of the magistrate, to see that the public burthens be equally borne. Furthermore, since what is brought by the subjects to public use, is nothing else but the price of their bought peace, it is good reason, that they who equally share in the peace, should also pay an equal part, either by contributing their monies or their labours to the commonweal. Now it is the law of nature, (by art. 15, chap. III), that every man in distributing right to others, do carry himself equal to

all. Wherefore rulers are by the natural law obliged to lay the burthens of the commonweal equally on their subjects.

11. Now in this place we understand an equality, not of money, but of burthen, that is to say, an equality of reason between the burthens and the benefits. For although all equally enjoy peace, yet the benefits springing from thence are not equal to all; for some get greater possessions, others less; and again, some consume less, others more. It may therefore be demanded whether subjects ought to contribute to the public, according to the rate of what they gain, or of what they spend, that is to say, whether the persons must be taxed, so as to pay contribution according to their wealth, or the goods themselves, that every man contribute according to what he spends. But if we consider, where monies are raised according to wealth, there they who have made equal gain, have not equal possessions, because that one preserves what he hath got by frugality, another wastes it by luxury, and therefore equally rejoicing in the benefit of peace, they do not equally sustain the burthens of the commonweal: and on the other side, where the goods themselves are taxed, there every man, while he spends his private goods, in the very act of consuming them he undiscernably pays part due to the commonweal, according to, not what he hath, but what by the benefit of the realm he hath had. It is no more to be doubted, but that the former way of commanding monies is against equity, and therefore against the duty of rulers; the latter is agreeable to reason, and the exercise of their authority.

12. In the third place we said, that that trouble of mind which riseth from ambition was offensive to public peace. For there are some who seeming to themselves to be wiser than others, and more sufficient for the managing of affairs than they who at present do govern, when they can no otherwise declare how profitable their virtue would prove to the common-

weal, they show it, by harming it. But because ambition and greediness of honours cannot be rooted out of the minds of men, it is not the duty of rulers to endeavour it; but by constant application of rewards and punishments, they may so order it, that men may know that the way to honour is, not by contempt of the present government, nor by factions and the popular air, but by the contraries. They are good men who observe the decrees, the laws, and rights of their fathers. If with a constant order we saw these adorned with honours, but the factious punished and had in contempt by those who bear command, there would be more ambition to obey, than withstand. Notwithstanding, it so happens sometimes, that as we must stroke a horse by reason of his too much fierceness, so a stiff-necked subject must be flattered for fear of his power; but as that happens when the rider, so this, when the commander is in danger of falling. But we speak here of those whose authority and power is entire. Their duty (I say) it is to cherish obedient subjects, and to depress the factious all they can; nor can the public power be otherwise preserved, nor the subjects' quiet without it.

13. But if it be the duty of princes to restrain the factious, much more does it concern them to dissolve and dissipate the factions themselves. Now I call a faction, a multitude of subjects gathered together, either by mutual contracts among themselves, or by the power of some one, without his or their authority who bear the supreme rule. A faction, therefore, is as it were a city in a city; for as by an union of men in the state of nature a city receives its being, so by a new union of subjects, there ariseth a faction. According to this definition, a multitude of subjects who have bound themselves simply to obey any foreign prince or subject, or have made any pacts or leagues of mutual defence between themselves against all men, not excepting those who have the supreme power in the

city, is a faction. Also favour with the vulgar, if it be so great, that by it an army may be raised, except public caution be given, either by hostages or some other pledges, contains faction in it. The same may be said of private wealth, if it exceed, because all things obey money. Forasmuch therefore as it is true, that the state of cities among themselves is natural and hostile, those princes who permit factions, do as much as if they received an enemy within their walls, which is contrary to the subjects' safety, and therefore also against the law of nature.

14. There are two things necessary to the enriching of the subjects, labour and thrift; there is also a third which helps, to wit, the natural increase of the earth and water; and there is a fourth too, namely, the militia, which sometimes augments, but more frequently lessens the subjects' stock. The two first only are necessary. For a city constituted in an island of the sea, no greater than will serve for dwelling, may grow rich without sowing or fishing, by merchandize and handicrafts only; but there is no doubt, if they have a territory, but they may be richer with the same number, or equally rich, being a greater number. But the fourth, namely, the militia, was of old reckoned in the number of the gaining arts, under the notion of booting or taking prey; and it was by mankind, (dispersed by families) before the constitution of civil societies, accounted just and honourable. For preying is nothing else but a war waged with small forces. And great commonweals, namely, that of Rome and Athens, by the spoils of war, foreign tribute, and the territories they have purchased by their arms, have sometimes so improved the commonwealth, that they have not only not required any public monies from the poorer sort of subjects, but have also divided to each of them both monies and lands. But this kind of increase of riches is not to be brought into rule and fashion. For the militia, in order

to profit, is like a die wherewith many lose their estates, but few improve them. Since therefore there are three things only, the fruits of the earth and water, labour, and thrift, which are expedient for the enriching of subjects, the duty of commanders in chief shall be conversant only about those three. For the first, those laws will be useful which countenance the arts that improve the increase of the earth and water, such as are husbandry and fishing. For the second, all laws against idleness, and such as quicken industry, are profitable; the art of navigation (by help whereof the commodities of the whole world, bought almost by labour only, are brought into one city) and the mechanics, (under which I comprehend all the arts of the most excellent workmen) and the mathematical sciences, the fountains of navigatory and mechanic employments, are held in due esteem and honour. For the third, those laws are useful, whereby all inordinate expense, as well in meats as in clothes, and universally in all things which are consumed with usage, is forbidden. Now because such laws are beneficial to the ends above specified, it belongs also to the office of supreme magistrates to establish them.

15. The liberty of subjects consists not in being exempt from the laws of the city, or that they who have the supreme power cannot make what laws they have a mind to. But because all the motions and actions of subjects are never circumscribed by laws, nor can be, by reason of their variety, it is necessary that there be infinite cases, which are neither commanded, nor prohibited, but every man may either do, or not do them, as he lists himself. In these, each man is said to enjoy his liberty; and in this sense liberty is to be understood in this place, namely, for that part of natural right, which is granted and left to subjects by the civil laws. As water inclosed on all hands with banks, stands still and corrupts; having no bounds, it spreads too largely, and the more passages it finds, the more

freely it takes its current; so subjects, if they might do nothing without the commands of the law would grow dull and unwieldy, if all, they would be dispersed, and the more is left undetermined by the laws, the more liberty they enjoy. Both extremes are faulty; for laws were not invented to take away, but to direct men's actions, even as nature ordained the banks, not to stay, but to guide the course of the stream. The measure of this liberty is to be taken from the subjects' and the city's good. Wherefore, in the first place, it is against the charge of those who command and have the authority of making laws, that there should be more laws than necessarily serve for good of the magistrate and his subjects. For since men are wont commonly to debate what to do, or not to do, by natural reason rather than any knowledge of the laws, where there are more laws than can easily be remembered, and whereby such things are forbidden, as reason of itself prohibits not of necessity, they must through ignorance, without the least evil intention, fall within the compass of laws, as gins laid to entrap their harmless liberty, which supreme commanders are bound to preserve for their subjects by the laws of nature.

16. It is a great part of that liberty, which is harmless to civil government, and necessary for each subject to live happily, that there be no penalties dreaded, but what they may both foresee and look for; and this is done, where there are either no punishments at all defined by the laws, or greater not required than are defined. Where there are none defined, there he that hath first broken the law, expects an indefinite or arbitrary punishment; and his fear is supposed boundless, because it relates to an unbounded evil. Now the law of nature commands them who are not subject to any civil laws, (by what we have said in chap. III. art. II) and therefore supreme commanders, that in taking revenge and punishing, they must not so much regard the past evil as the future good;

and they sin, if they entertain any other measure in arbitrary punishment, than the public benefit. But where the punishment is defined, either by a law prescribed, as when it is set down in plain words, that he that shall do thus or thus, shall suffer so and so; or by practice, as when the penalty, (not by any law prescribed, but arbitrary from the beginning) is afterward determined by the punishment of the first delinquent (for natural equity commands that equal transgressors be equally punished); there to impose a greater penalty than is defined by the law, is against the law of nature. For the end of punishment is not to compel the will of man, but to fashion it, and to make it such as he would have it who hath set the penalty. And deliberation is nothing else but a weighing, as it were in scales, the conveniences and inconveniences of the fact we are attempting; where that which is more weighty, doth necessarily according to its inclination prevail with us. If therefore the legislator doth set a less penalty on a crime, than will make our fear more considerable with us than our lust, that excess of lust above the fear of punishment, whereby sin is committed, is to be attributed to the legislator, that is to say, to the supreme; and therefore if he inflict a greater punishment, than himself hath determined in his laws, he punisheth that in another, in which he sinned himself.

17. It pertains therefore to the harmless and necessary liberty of subjects, that every man may without fear enjoy the rights which are allowed him by the laws. For it is in vain to have our own distinguished by the laws from another's, if by wrong judgment, robbery, or theft, they may be again confounded. But it falls out so, that these do happen where judges are corrupted. For the fear whereby men are deterred from doing evil, ariseth not from hence, namely, because penalties are set, but because they are executed. For we esteem the future by what is past, seldom expecting what seldom

happens. If therefore judges, corrupted either by gifts, favour, or even by pity itself, do often forbear the execution of the penalties due by the law, and by that means put wicked men in hope to pass unpunished: honest subjects encompassed with murderers, thieves, and knaves, will not have the liberty to converse freely with each other, nor scarce to stir abroad without hazard; nay, the city itself is dissolved, and every man's right of protecting himself at his own will returns to him. The law of nature therefore gives this precept to supreme commanders, that they not only do righteousness themselves, but that they also by penalties cause the judges, by them appointed, to do the same; that is to say, that they hearken to the complaints of their subjects; and as oft as need requires make choice of some extraordinary judges, who may hear the matter debated concerning the ordinary ones.

CHAPTER XIV

OF LAWS AND TRESPASSES

1. THEY who less seriously consider the force of words, do sometimes confound law with counsel, sometimes with covenant, sometimes with right. They confound law with counsel, who think that it is the duty of monarchs not only to give ear to their counsellors, but also to obey them, as though it were in vain to take counsel, unless it were also followed. We must fetch the distinction between counsel and law, from the difference between counsel and command. Now counsel is a precept in which the reason of my obeying it, is taken from the thing itself which is advised; but command is a precept, in which the cause of my obedience depends on the will of the commander. For it is not properly said, thus I will and thus I command, except the will stand for a reason. Now when obedience is yielded to the laws, not for the thing itself, but by reason of the adviser's will, the law is not a counsel, but a command, and is defined thus: law is the command of that person (whether man or court) whose precept contains in it the reason of obedience; as the precepts of God in regard of men, of magistrates in respect of their subjects, and universally of all the powerful in respect of them who cannot resist, may be termed their laws. Law and counsel therefore differ many ways. Law belongs to him who hath power over them whom he adviseth; counsel to them who have no power. To follow what is prescribed by law, is duty; what by counsel, is free-will. Counsel is directed to his end that receives it; law, to his that gives it. Counsel is given to none but the willing;

law even to the unwilling. To conclude, the right of the counsellor is made void by the will of him to whom he gives counsel; the right of the law-giver is not abrogated at the pleasure of him who hath a law imposed.

2. They confound law and covenant, who conceive the laws to be nothing else but certain ὁμολογήματα, or forms of living determined by the common consent of men. Among whom is Aristotle, who defines law on this manner; Νόμός ἐστι λόγος ὡρισμένος καθ' ὁμολογίαν κοινὴν πόλεως, μηνύων πῶς δεῖ πράττειν ἕκαστα: that is to say, law is a speech, limited according to the common consent of the city, declaring every thing that we ought to do; which definition is not simply of law, but of the civil law. For it is manifest that the divine laws sprang not from the consent of men, nor yet the laws of nature. For if they had their original from the consent of men, they might also by the same consent be abrogated; but they are unchangeable. But indeed, that is no right definition of a civil law. For in that place, a city is taken either for one civil person, having one will, or for a multitude of men, who have each of them the liberty of their private wills. If for one person, those words common consent are ill-placed here; for one person hath no common consent. Neither ought he to have said, declaring what was needful to be done, but commanding; for what the city declares, it commands its subjects. He therefore by a city understood a multitude of men, declaring by common consent (imagine it a writing confirmed by votes) some certain forms of living. But these are nothing else but some mutual contracts which oblige not any man (and therefore are no laws) before that a supreme power being constituted, which can compel, have sufficient remedy against the rest, who otherwise are not likely to keep them. Laws therefore, according to this definition of Aristotle, are nothing else but naked and weak contracts, which then at

length, when there is one who by right doth exercise the supreme power, shall either become laws or no laws at his will and pleasure. Wherefore he confounds contracts with laws, which he ought not to have done; for contract is a promise, law a command. In contracts we say, I will do this; in laws, do this. Contracts oblige us;* laws tie us fast, being obliged. A contract obligeth of itself; the law holds the party obliged by virtue of the universal contract of yielding obedience. Therefore in contract, it is first determined what is to be done, before we are obliged to do it; but in law, we are first obliged to perform, and what is to be done is determined afterwards. Aristotle therefore ought to have defined a civil law thus: a civil law is a speech limited by the will of the city, commanding everything behoveful to be done, which is the same with that we have given above, in chap. vi. art. 9, to wit, that the civil laws are the command of him (whether man or court of men) who is endued with supreme power in the city, concerning the future actions of his subjects.

3. They confound laws with right, who continue still to do what is permitted by divine right, notwithstanding it be forbidden by the civil law. That which is prohibited by the divine law, cannot be permitted by the civil, neither can that which is commanded by the divine law, be prohibited by the civil. Notwithstanding, that which is permitted by the divine right, that is to say, that which may be done by divine right, doth no whit hinder why the same may not be forbidden by the civil laws; for inferior laws may restrain the liberty allowed

---

*To be obliged, and to be tied being obliged, seems to some men to be one and the same thing, and that therefore here seems to be some distinction in words, but none indeed. More clearly therefore, I say thus, that a man is obliged by his contracts, that is, that he ought to perform for his promise sake; but that the law ties him being obliged, that is to say, it compels him to make good his promise, for fear of the punishment appointed by the law.

by the superior, although they cannot enlarge them. Now natural liberty is a right not constituted, but allowed by the laws. For the laws being removed, our liberty is absolute. This is first restrained by the natural and divine laws; the residue is bounded by the civil law; and what remains, may again be restrained by the constitutions of particular towns and societies. There is great difference therefore between law and right. For law is a fetter, right is freedom, and they differ like contraries.

4. All law may be divided, first according to the diversity of its authors into divine and human. The divine, according to the two ways whereby God hath made known his will unto men, is two-fold, natural (or moral) and positive. Natural is that which God hath declared to all men by his eternal word born with them, to wit, their natural reason; and this is that law, which in this whole book I have endeavoured to unfold. Positive is that, which God hath revealed to us by the word of prophecy, wherein he hath spoken unto men as a man. Such are the laws which he gave to the Jews concerning their government and divine worship; and they may be termed the divine civil laws, because they were peculiar to the civil government of the Jews, his peculiar people. Again, the natural law may be divided into that of men, which alone hath obtained the title of the law of nature, and that of cities, which may be called that of nations, but vulgarly it is termed the right of nations. The precepts of both are alike. But because cities once instituted do put on the personal proprieties of men, that law, which speaking of the duty of single men we call natural, being applied to whole cities and nations, is called the right of nations. And the same elements of natural law and right, which have hitherto been spoken of, being transferred to whole cities and nations, may be taken for the elements of the laws and right of nations.

5. All human law is civil. For the state of men considered out of civil society, is hostile, in which, because one is not subject to another, there are no other laws, beside the dictates of natural reason, which is the divine law. But in civil government the city only, that is to say, that man or court to whom the supreme power of the city is committed, is the legislator, and the laws of the city are civil. The civil laws may be divided, according to the diversity of their subject matter, into sacred or secular. Sacred are those which pertain to religion, that is to say, to the ceremonies and worship of God (to wit, what persons, things, places, are to be consecrated, and in what fashion, what opinions concerning the Deity are to be taught publicly, and with what words, and in what order supplications are to be made, and the like), and are not determined by any divine positive law. For the civil sacred laws are the human laws (which are also called ecclesiastical) concerning things sacred; but the secular, under a general notion, are usually called the civil laws.

6. Again, the civil law (according to the two offices of the legislator, whereof one is to judge, the other to constrain men to acquiesce to his judgments) hath two parts; the one distributive, the other vindicative or penal. By the distributive it is, that every man hath his proper right, that is to say, it sets forth rules for all things, whereby we may know what is properly ours, what another man's; so as others may not hinder us from the free use and enjoyment of our own; and we may not interrupt others in the quiet possession of theirs; and what is lawful for every man to do or omit, and what is not lawful. Vindicative is that whereby it is defined what punishment shall be inflicted on them who break the law.

7. Now distributive and vindicative are not two several species of the laws, but two parts of the same law. For if the law should say no more, but (for example) whatsoever you

take with your net in the sea, be it yours, it is in vain. For although another should take that away from you which you have caught, it hinders not, but that it still remains yours. For in the state of nature where all things are common to all, yours and others' are all one, insomuch as what the law defines to be yours, was yours even before the law, and after the law ceases not to be yours, although in another man's possession. Wherefore the law doth nothing, unless it be understood to be so yours, as all other men be forbidden to interrupt your free use and secure enjoyment of it at all times, according to your own will and pleasure. For this is that which is required to a propriety of goods, not that a man may be able to use them, but to use them alone, which is done by prohibiting others to be an hinderance to him. But in vain do they also prohibit any men, who do not withal strike a fear of punishment into them. In vain therefore is the law, unless it contain both parts, that which forbids injuries to be done, and that which punisheth the doers of them. The first of them which is called distributive, is prohibitory, and speaks to all; the second which is styled vindicative or penary, is mandatory, and only speaks to public ministers.

8. From hence also we may understand, that every civil law hath a penalty annexed to it, either explicitly or implicitly. For where the penalty is not defined, neither by any writing, nor by example of any who hath suffered the punishment of the transgressed law, there the penalty is understood to be arbitrary, namely, to depend on the will of the legislator, that is to say, of the supreme commander. For in vain is that law which may be broken without punishment.

9. Now because it comes from the civil laws, both that every man have his proper right, and distinguished from another's, and also that he is forbidden to invade another's rights, it follows that these precepts: Thou shalt not refuse to

give the honour defined by the laws unto thy parents: Thou shalt not kill the man whom the laws forbid thee to kill: Thou shalt avoid all copulation forbidden by the laws: Thou shalt not take away another's goods against the lord's will: Thou shalt not frustrate the laws and judgments by false testimony: are civil laws. The natural laws command the same things, but implicitly; for the law of nature (as hath been said in chap. III. art. 2) commands us to keep contracts, and therefore also to perform obedience, when we have covenanted obedience, and to abstain from another's goods, when it is determined by the civil law what belongs to another. But all subjects (by chap. VI. art. 13) do covenant to obey his commands who hath the supreme power, that is to say, the civil laws, in the very constitution of government, even before it is possible to break them. For the law of nature did oblige in the state of nature, where first (because nature hath given all things to all men) nothing did properly belong to another, and therefore it was not possible to invade another's right; next, where all things were common, and therefore all carnal copulations lawful; thirdly, where was the state of war, and therefore lawful to kill; fourthly, where all things were determined by every man's own judgment, and therefore paternal respects also; lastly, where there were no public judgments, and therefore no use of bearing witness, either true or false.

10. Seeing therefore our obligation to observe those laws is more ancient than the promulgation of the laws themselves, as being contained in the very constitution of the city, by the virtue of the natural law which forbids breach of covenant, the law of nature commands us to keep all the civil laws. For where we are tied to obedience, before we know what will be commanded us, there we are universally tied to obey in all things. Whence it follows, that no civil law whatsoever, which tends not to a reproach of the Deity (in respect of whom

cities themselves have no right of their own, and cannot be said to make laws), can possibly be against the law of nature. For though the law of nature forbid theft, adultery, &c, yet if the civil law command us to invade anything, that invasion is not theft, adultery, &c. For when the Lacedæmonians of old permitted their youths by a certain law, to take away other men's goods, they commanded that these goods should not be accounted other men's, but their own who took them; and therefore such surreptions were no thefts. In like manner, copulations of heathen sexes, according to their laws, were lawful marriages.

11. It is necessary to the essence of a law, that the subjects be acquainted with two things: first, what man or court hath the supreme power, that is to say, the right of making laws; secondly, what the law itself says. For he that neither knew either to whom or what he is tied to, cannot obey, and by consequence is in such a condition, as if he were not tied at all. I say not that it is necessary to the essence of a law, that either one or the other be perpetually known, but only that it be once known. And if the subject afterward forget either the right he hath who made the law, or the law itself, that makes him no less tied to obey, since he might have remembered it, had he had a will to obey.

12. The knowledge of the legislator depends on the subject himself; for the right of making laws could not be conferred on any man without his own consent and covenant, either expressed or supposed; expressed, when from the beginning the citizens do themselves constitute a form of governing the city, or when by promise they submit themselves to the dominion of any one; or supposed at least, as when they make use of the benefit of the realm and laws for their protection and conservation against others. For to whose dominion we require our fellow subjects to yield obedience for

our good, his dominion we acknowledge to be legitimate by that very request. And therefore ignorance of the power of making laws, can never be a sufficient excuse; for every man knows what he hath done himself.

13. The knowledge of the laws depends on the legislator, who must publish them, for otherwise they are not laws. For law is the command of the law-maker, and his command is the declaration of his will; it is not therefore a law, except the will of the law-maker be declared, which is done by promulgation. Now in promulgation two things must be manifest, whereof one is, that he or they who publish a law, either have a right themselves to make laws, or that they do it by authority derived from him or them who have it; the other is the sense of the law itself. Now, that the first, namely, published laws, proceed from him who hath the supreme command, cannot be manifest (speaking exactly and philo-sophically) to any, but them who have received them from the mouth of the commander. The rest believe; but the rea-sons of their belief are so many, that it is scarce possible they should not believe. And truly in a democratical city where every one may be present at the making of laws if he will, he that shall be absent, must believe those that were present. But in monarchies and aristocracies, because it is granted but to few to be present, and openly to hear the commands of the monarch or the nobles, it was necessary to bestow a power on those few of publishing them to the rest. And thus we believe those to be the edicts and decrees of princes, which are propounded to us for such, either by the writings or voices of them whose office it is to publish them. But yet, when we have these causes of belief, that we have seen the prince or supreme counsel constantly use such counsellors, secretaries, publishers, and seals, and the like arguments for the declaring of his will; that he never took any authority

from them; that they have been punished who not giving credit to such like promulgations have transgressed the law; not only he who thus believing shall obey the edicts and decrees set forth by them, is everywhere excused, but he that not believing shall not yield obedience, is punished. For the constant permission of these things is a manifest sign enough, and evident declaration of the commander's will; provided there be nothing contained in the law, edict, or decree, derogatory from his supreme power. For it is not to be imagined that he would have aught taken from his power by any of his officers as long as he retains a will to govern. Now the sense of the law, when there is any doubt made of it, is to be taken from them to whom the supreme authority hath committed the knowledge of causes or judgments; for to judge is nothing else than by interpretation to apply the laws to particular cases. Now we may know who they are that have this office granted them, in the same manner as we know who they be that have authority given them to publish laws.

14. Again the civil law, according to its two-fold manner of publishing, is of two sorts, written and unwritten. By written, I understand that which wants a voice, or some other sign of the will of the legislator, that it may become a law. For all kind of laws are of the same age with mankind, both in nature and time, and therefore of more antiquity than the invention of letters, and the art of writing. Wherefore not a writing, but a voice is necessary for a written law; this alone is requisite to the being, that to the remembrance of a law. For we read, that before letters were found out for the help of memory, that laws, contracted into metre, were wont to be sung. The unwritten is that which wants no other publishing than the voice of nature or natural reason; such are the laws of nature. For the natural law, although it be distinguished from the civil, forasmuch as it commands the will,

yet so far forth as it relates to our actions, it is civil. For example, this same, thou shalt not covet, which only appertains to the mind, is a natural law only; but this, thou shalt not invade, is both natural and civil. For seeing it is impossible to prescribe such universal rules, whereby all future contentions, which perhaps are infinite, may be determined, it is to be understood that in all cases not mentioned by the written laws, the law of natural equity is to be followed, which commands us to distribute equally to equals; and this by the virtue of the civil law, which also punisheth those who knowingly and willingly do actually transgress the laws of nature.

15. These things being understood, it appears first, that the laws of nature, although they were described in the books of some philosophers, are not for that reason to be termed written laws: and that the writings of the interpreters of the laws, were no laws, for want of the supreme authority; nor yet those orations of the wise, that is to say, judges, but so far forth as by the consent of the supreme power they part into custom; and that then they are to be received among the written laws, not for the custom's sake (which by its own force doth not constitute a law), but for the will of the supreme commander, which appears in this, that he hath suffered his sentence, whether equal or unequal, to pass into custom.

16. Sin, in its largest signification, comprehends every deed, word, and thought against right reason. For every man, by reasoning, seeks out the means to the end which he propounds to himself. If therefore he reason right (that is to say, beginning from most evident principles he makes a discourse out of consequences continually necessary), he will proceed in a most direct way. Otherwise he will go astray, that is to say, he will either do, say, or endeavour somewhat against his

proper end, which when he hath done, he will indeed in reasoning be said to have erred, but in action and will to have sinned. For sin follows error, just as the will doth the understanding. And this is the most general acception of the word, under which is contained every imprudent action, whether against the law, as to overthrow another man's house, or not against the law, as to build his own upon the sand.

17. But when we speak of the laws, the word sin is taken in a more strict sense, and signifies not every thing done against right reason, but that only which is blameable, and therefore is called *malum culpæ,* the evil of fault. But yet if anything be culpable, it is not presently to be termed a sin or fault, but only if it be blameable with reason. We must therefore enquire what it is to be blameable with reason, what against reason. Such is the nature of man, that every one calls that good which he desires, and evil which he eschews. And therefore through the diversity of our affections, it happens that one counts that good, which another counts evil; and the same man what now he esteemed for good, he immediately after looks on as evil: and the same thing which he calls good in himself, he terms evil in another. For we all measure good and evil by the pleasure or pain we either feel at present, or expect hereafter. Now seeing the prosperous actions of enemies (because they increase their honours, goods, and power) and of equals, (by reason of that strife of honours which is among them), both seem and are irksome, and therefore evil to all; and men use to repute those evil, that is to say, to lay some fault to their charge from whom they receive evil; it is impossible to be determined by the consent of single men whom the same things do not please and displease, what actions are, and what not to be blamed. They may agree indeed in some certain general things, as that theft, adultery, and the like are sins, as if they should say that all men account

those things evil to which they have given names which are usually taken in an evil sense. But we demand not whether theft be a sin, but what is to be termed theft, and so concerning others, in like manner. Forasmuch therefore as in so great a diversity of censurers, what is by reason blameable, is not to be measured by the reason of one man more than another, because of the equality of human nature, and there are no other reasons in being, but only those of particular men, and that of the city, it follows, that the city is to determine what with reason is culpable. So as a fault, that is to say, a sin, is that which a man does, omits, says, or wills, against the reason of the city, that is, contrary to the laws.

18. But a man may do somewhat against the laws through human infirmity, although he desire to fulfil them; and yet his action, as being against the laws, is rightly blamed, and called a sin. But there are some who neglect the laws; and as oft as any hope of gain and impunity doth appear to them, no conscience of contracts and betrothed faith can withhold them from their violation. Not only the deeds, but even the minds of these men are against the laws. They who sin only through infirmity, are good men even when they sin; but these, even when they do not sin, are wicked. For though both the action and the mind be repugnant to the laws, yet those repugnances are distinguished by different appellations. For the irregularity of the action is called ἀδίκημα, unjust deed; that of the mind ἀδικία and κακία, injustice and malice; that is the infirmity of a disturbed soul, this the pravity of a sober mind.

19. But seeing there is no sin which is not against some law, and that there is no law which is not the command of him who hath the supreme power, and that no man hath a supreme power which is not bestowed on him by our own consent; in what manner will he be said to sin, who either denies that there is a God, or that he governs the world, or casts any

other reproach upon him? For he will say, that he never submitted his will to God's will, not conceiving him so much as
to have any being, and granting that his opinion were erroneous, and therefore also a sin, yet were it to be numbered among
those of imprudence or ignorance, which by right cannot be
punished. This speech seems so far forth to be admitted, that
though this kind of sin be the greatest and most hurtful, yet
is it to be referred to sins of imprudence; * but that it should
be excused by imprudence or ignorance, is absurd. For the
atheist is punished either immediately by God himself, or by
kings constituted under God; not as a subject is punished by
a king, because he keeps not the laws, but as one enemy
by another, because he would not accept of the laws; that is to

* Many find fault that I have referred atheism to imprudence, and not
to injustice; yea by some it is taken so, as if I had not declared myself
an enemy bitter enough against atheists. They object further, that since
I had elsewhere said that it might be known there is a God by natural
reason, I ought to have acknowledged that they sin at least against the
law of nature, and therefore are not only guilty of imprudence, but injustice too. But I am so much an enemy to atheists, that I have both dili-
gently sought for, and vehemently desired to find some law whereby I
might condemn them of injustice. But when I found none, I inquired
next what name God himself did give to men so detested by him. Now
God speaks thus of the atheist: The fool hath said in his heart, there is
no God. Wherefore I placed their sin in that rank which God himself
refers to. Next I show them to be enemies of God. But I conceive the
name of an enemy to be sometimes somewhat sharper, than that of an
unjust man. Lastly, I affirm that they may under that notion be justly
punished both by God, and supreme magistrates, and therefore by no
means excuse or extenuate this sin. Now that I have said that it might be
known by natural reason that there is a God, is so to be understood, not
as if I had meant that all men might know this, except they think that
because Archimedes by natural reason found out what proportion the
circle hath to the square, it follows thence, that every one of the vulgar
could have found out as much. I say therefore, that although it may
be known to some by the light of reason that there is a God; yet men
that are continually engaged in pleasures or seeking of riches and honour,
also men that are not wont to reason aright, or cannot do it, or care not
to do it, lastly, fools, in which number are atheists, cannot know this.

say, by the right of war, as the giants warring against God. For whosoever are not subject either to some common lord, or one to another, are enemies among themselves.

20. Seeing that from the virtue of the covenant whereby each subject is tied to the other to perform absolute and universal obedience (such as is defined above, chap. VI. art. 13) to the city, that is to say, to the sovereign power, whether that be one man or council, there is an obligation derived to observe each one of the civil laws, so that that covenant contains in itself all the laws at once; it is manifest that the subject who shall renounce the general covenant of obedience, doth at once renounce all the laws. Which trespass is so much worse than any other one sin, by how much to sin always, is worse than to sin once. And this is that sin which is called treason; and it is a word or deed whereby the citizen or subject declares, that he will no longer obey that man or court to whom the supreme power of the city is entrusted. And the subject declares this same will of his by deed, when he either doth or endeavours to do violence to the sovereign's person, or to them who execute his commands. Of which sort are traitors, regicides, and such as take up arms against the city, or during a war fly to the enemy's side. And they show the same will in word, who flatly deny that themselves or other subjects are tied to any such kind of obedience, either in the whole, as he who should say that we must not obey him (keeping the obedience which we owe to God entire) simply, absolutely, and universally; or in part, as he who should say, that he had no right to wage war at his own will, to make peace, enlist soldiers, levy monies, electing magistrates and public ministers, enacting laws, deciding controversies, setting penalties, or doing aught else without which the state cannot stand. And these and the like words and deeds are treason by the natural, not the civil law. But it may so happen, that some action which, before

the civil law was made, was not treason, yet will become such, if it be done afterwards. As if it be declared by the law, that it shall be accounted for a sign of renouncing public obedience (that is to say, for treason) if any man shall coin monies, or forge the privy-seal, he that after that declaration shall do this, will be no less guilty of treason than the other. Yet he sins less, because he breaks not all the laws at once, but one law only. For the law by calling that treason which by nature is not so, doth indeed by right set a more odious name, and perhaps a more grievous punishment, on the guilty persons; but it makes not the sin itself more grievous.

21. But that sin which by the law of nature is treason, is a transgression of the natural, not the civil law. For since our obligation to civil obedience, by virtue whereof the civil laws are valid, is before all civil law, and the sin of treason is naturally nothing else but the breach of that obligation; it follows, that by the sin of treason, that law is broken which preceded the civil law, to wit, the natural, which forbids us to violate covenants and betrothed faith. But if some sovereign prince should set forth a law on this manner, thou shalt not rebel, he would effect just nothing. For except subjects were before obliged to obedience, that is to say, not to rebel, all law is of no force. Now the obligation which obligeth to what we were before obliged to, is superfluous.

22. Hence it follows, that rebels, traitors, and all others convicted of treason, are punished not by civil, but natural right, that is to say, not as civil subjects, but as enemies to the government, not by the right of sovereignty and dominion, but by the right of war.

23. There are some who think that those acts which are done against the law, when the punishment is determined by the law itself, are expiated, if the punished willingly undergo the punishment; and that they are not guilty before God of

breaking the natural law (although by breaking the civil laws, we break the natural too, which command us to keep the civil) who have suffered the punishment which the law required; as if by the law, the fact were not prohibited, but a punishment were set instead of a price, whereby a license might be bought of doing what the law forbids. By the same reason they might infer too, that no transgression of the law were a sin, but that every man might enjoy the liberty which he hath bought by his own peril. But we must know that the words of the law may be understood in a two-fold sense, the one as containing two parts (as hath been declared above in art. 7), namely, that of absolutely prohibiting, as, thou shall not do this; and revenging, as, he that doth this, shall be punished; the other, as containing a condition, for example, thou shalt not do this thing, unless thou wilt suffer punishment; and thus the law forbids not simply, but conditionally. If it be understood in the first sense, he that doth it sins, because he doth what the law forbids to be done; if in the second, he sins not, because he cannot be said to do what is forbidden him, that performs the condition. For in the first sense, all men are forbidden to do it; in the second, they only who keep themselves from the punishment. In the first sense, the vindicative part of the law obligeth not the guilty, but the magistrate to require punishment; in the second, he himself that owes the punishment is obliged to exact it, to the payment whereof, if it be capital or otherwise grievous, he cannot be obliged. But in what sense the law is to be taken, depends on the will of him who hath the sovereignty. When there is therefore any doubt of the meaning of the law, since we are sure they sin not who do it not, it will be sin if we do it, howsoever the law may afterward be explained. For to do that which a man doubts whether it be a sin or not, when he hath freedom to forbear it, is a contempt of the laws, and therefore, by chap. III. art. 28, a sin against the law of nature. Vain therefore is that same distinction of obedience into active and passive, as if that could be expiated by penalties constituted by human decrees, which is a sin against the law of nature, which is the law of God; or as though they sinned not, who sin at their own peril.

Part III: RELIGION

Chapter XV

Of the Kingdom of God by Nature

1. We have already in the foregoing chapters, proved both by reason and testimonies of holy writ, that the estate of nature, that is to say, of absolute liberty, such as is theirs, who neither govern nor are governed, is an anarchy or hostile state; that the precepts whereby to avoid this state, are the laws of nature; that there can be no civil government without a sovereign; and that they who have gotten this sovereign command must be obeyed simply, that is to say, in all things which repugn not the commandments of God. There is this one thing only wanting to the complete understanding of all civil duty, and that is, to know which are the laws and commandments of God. For else we cannot tell whether that which the civil power commands us, be against the laws of God, or not; whence it must necessarily happen, that either by too much obedience to the civil authority, we become stubborn against the divine Majesty; or for fear of sinning against God, we run into disobedience against the civil power. To avoid both these rocks, it is necessary to know the divine laws. Now because the knowledge of the laws depends on the knowledge of the kingdom, we must in what follows speak somewhat concerning the kingdom of God.

2. *The Lord is king, the earth may be glad thereof;* saith the psalmist, (Psalm xcvii. 1). And again the same psalmist, (Psalm xcix. 1): *The Lord is king, be the people never so impatient; he sitteth between the cherubims, be the earth never so unquiet;* to wit, whether men will or not, God is the king

175

over all the earth, nor is he moved from his throne, if there be any who deny either his existence or his providence. Now although God govern all men so by his power, that none can do anything which he would not have done: yet this, to speak properly and accurately, is not to reign. For he is said to reign, who rules not by acting, but speaking, that is to say, by precepts and threatenings. And therefore we count not inanimate nor irrational bodies for subjects in the kingdom of God, although they be subordinate to the divine power; because they understand not the commands and threats of God; nor yet the atheists, because they believe not that there is a God; nor yet those who believing there is a God, do not yet believe that he rules these inferior things; for even these, although they be governed by the power of God, yet do they not acknowledge any of his commands, nor stand in awe of his threats. Those only therefore are supposed to belong to God's kingdom, who acknowledge him to be the governor of all things, and that he hath given his commands to men, and appointed punishments for the transgressors. The rest we must not call subjects, but enemies of God.

3. But none are said to govern by commands, but they who openly declare them to those who are governed by them. For the commands of the rulers are the laws of the ruled; but laws they are not, if not perspicuously published, in so much as all excuse of ignorance may be taken away. Men indeed publish their laws by word or voice, neither can they make their will universally known any other way. But God's laws are declared after a threefold manner: first, by the tacit dictates of right reason; next, by immediate revelation, which is supposed to be done either by a supernatural voice, or by a vision or dream, or divine inspiration; thirdly, by the voice of one man whom God recommends to the rest, as worthy of belief, by the working of true miracles. Now he whose voice God thus

makes use of to signify his will unto others, is called a prophet. These three manners may be termed the threefold word of God, to wit, the rational word, the sensible word, and the word of prophecy. To which answer the three manners whereby we are said to hear God, right reasoning, sense, and faith. God's sensible word hath come but to few; neither hath God spoken to men by revelation except particularly to some, and to diverse diversely; neither have any laws of his kingdom been published on this manner unto any people.

4. And according to the difference which is between the rational word and the word of prophecy, we attribute a two-fold kingdom unto God: natural, in which he reigns by the dictates of right reason, and which is universal over all who acknowledge the divine power, by reason of that rational nature which is common to all; and prophetical, in which he rules also by the word of prophecy, which is peculiar, because he hath not given positive laws to all men, but to his peculiar people, and some certain men elected by him.

5. God in his natural kingdom hath a right to rule, and to punish those who break his laws, from his sole irresistible power. For all right over others is either from nature, or from contract. How the right of governing springs from contract, we have already showed in chap. VI. And the same right is derived from nature, in this very thing, that it is not by nature taken away. For when by nature all men had a right over all things, every man had a right of ruling over all as ancient as nature itself. But the reason why this was abolished among men, was no other but mutual fear, as hath been declared above in chap. II. art. 3; reason, namely, dictating that they must forego that right for the preservation of mankind, because the equality of men among themselves, according to their strength and natural powers, was necessarily accompanied with war, and with war joins the destruction of mankind. Now if

any man had so far exceeded the rest in power, that all of them with joined forces could not have resisted him, there had been no cause why he should part with that right which nature had given him. The right therefore of dominion over all the rest, would have remained with him, by reason of that excess of power whereby he could have preserved both himself and them. They therefore whose power cannot be resisted, and by consequence God Almighty, derives his right of sovereignty from the power itself. And as oft as God punisheth or slays a sinner, although he therefore punish him because he sinned, yet may we not say that he could not justly have punished or killed him although he had not sinned. Neither, if the will of God in punishing may perhaps have regard to some sin antecedent, doth it therefore follow, that the right of afflicting and killing depends not on divine power, but on men's sins.

6. That question made famous by the disputations of the ancients, why evil things befell the good, and good things the evil, is the same with this of ours, by what right God dispenseth good and evil things unto men. And with its difficulty, it not only staggers the faith of the vulgar concerning the divine providence, but also of philosophers, and which is more, even of holy men. Psalm lxxiii. 1, 2, 3: *Truly God is good to Israel, even to such as are of a clean heart; but as for me, my feet were almost gone, my steps had well nigh slipped. And why? I was grieved at the wicked; I do also see the ungodly in such prosperity.* And how bitterly did Job expostulate with God, that being just, he should yet be afflicted with so many calamities? God himself with open voice resolved this difficulty in the case of Job, and hath confirmed his right by arguments drawn not from Job's sin, but from his own power. For Job and his friends had argued so among themselves, that they would needs make him guilty, because he was punished; and he would reprove their accusation by arguments fetched from

his own innocence. But God, when he had heard both him and them, refutes his expostulation, not by condemning him of injustice or any sin, but by declaring his own power (Job xxxviii. 4): *Where wast thou* (says he) *when I laid the foundation of the earth, &c.* And for his friends, God pronounces himself angry against them (Job xlii. 7): *Because they had not spoken of him the thing that is right, like his servant Job.* Agreeable to this is that speech of our Saviour's in the man's case who was born blind, when, his disciples asking him whether he or his parents had sinned, that he was born blind, he answered, (John ix. 3): *Neither hath this man sinned, nor his parents; but that the works of God should be manifest in him.* For though it be said, (Rom. v. 12), *that death entered into the world by sin:* it follows not, but that God by his right might have made men subject to diseases and death, although they had never sinned, even as he hath made the other animals mortal and sickly, although they cannot sin.

7. Now if God have the right of sovereignty from his power, it is manifest, that the obligation of yielding him obedience lies on men by reason of their weakness.* For that obligation which rises from contract, of which we have spoken in chap. II, can have no place here, where the right of ruling (no covenant passing between) rises only from nature. But there are two species of natural obligation, one, when liberty is taken away by corporal impediments, according to which we say that heaven and earth, and all creatures, do obey the common laws of their creation; the other, when it is taken away by hope or

* If this shall seem hard to any man, I desire him with a silent thought to consider, if there were two Omnipotents, whether were bound to obey. I believe he will confess that neither is bound. If this be true, then it is also true what I have set down; that men are subject unto God, because they are not omnipotent. And truly our Saviour admonishing Paul, (who at that time was an enemy to the Church) that he should not kick against the pricks, seems to require obedience from him for this cause, because he had not power enough to resist.

fear, according to which the weaker, despairing of his own power to resist, cannot but yield to the stronger. From this last kind of obligation, that is to say, from fear, or conscience of our own weakness (in respect of the divine power), it comes to pass, that we are obliged to obey God in his natural kingdom; reason dictating to all, acknowledging the divine power and providence, that there is no kicking against the pricks.

8. Because the word of God, ruling by nature only, is supposed to be nothing else but right reason, and the laws of kings can be known by their word only, it is manifest that the laws of God, ruling by nature alone, are only the natural laws, namely, those which we have set down in chaps. ii and iii, and deduced from the dictates of reason, humility, equity, justice, mercy, and other moral virtues befriending peace, which pertain to the discharge of the duties of men one toward the other, and those which right reason shall dictate besides, concerning the honour and worship of the Divine Majesty. We need not repeat what those natural laws or moral virtues are; but we must see what honours and what divine worship, that is to say, what sacred laws, the same natural reason doth dictate.

9. Honour, to speak properly, is nothing else but an opinion of another's power joined with goodness; and to honour a man, is the same with highly esteeming him, and so honour is not in the party honoured, but in the honourer. Now three passions do necessarily follow honour thus placed in opinion; love, which refers to goodness; hope and fear, which regard power. And from these arise all outward actions, wherewith the powerful are appeased, and become propitious, and which are the effects, and therefore also the natural signs of honour itself. But the word honour is transferred also to those outward effects of honour; in which sense, we are said to honour him, of whose power we testify ourselves, either in word or deed,

to have a very great respect; insomuch as honour is the same
with worship. Now worship is an outward act, the sign of
inward honour; and whom we endeavour by our homage to
appease, if they be angry, or howsoever to make them favour-
able to us, we are said to worship.

10. All signs of the mind are either words or deeds; and
therefore all worship consists either in words or deeds. Now
both the one and the other are referred to three kinds; whereof
the first is praise, or public declaration of goodness; the second,
a public declaration of present power, which is to magnify,
μεγάλυνσις; the third is a public declaration of happiness, or
of power secure also for the future, which is called μακαρισμός.
I say that all kinds of honour may be discerned, not in words
only, but in deeds too. But we then praise and celebrate in
words, when we do it by way of proposition, or dogmatically,
that is to say, by attributes or titles, which may be termed
praising and celebrating categorically and plainly, as when
we declare him whom we honour to be liberal, strong, wise.
And then in deeds, when it is done by consequence, or by
hypothesis, or supposition, as by thanksgiving, which supposeth goodness; or by obedience, which supposeth power; or
by congratulation, which supposeth happiness.

11. Now whether we desire to praise a man in words or
deeds, we shall find some things which signify honour with
all men, such as among attributes, are the general words of
virtues and powers, which cannot be taken in ill sense, as
good, fair, strong, just, and the like; and among actions, obedience, thanksgiving, prayers, and others of that kind, by which
an acknowledgment of virtue and power is ever understood.
Others, which signify honour but with some, and scorn with
others, or else neither; such as in attributes, are those words
which, according to the diversity of opinions, are diversely referred to virtues or vices, to honest or dishonest things. As

that a man slew his enemy, that he fled, that he is a philosopher, or an orator, and the like, which with some are had in honour, with others in contempt. In deeds, such as depend on the custom of the place, or prescriptions of civil laws, as in saluting to be bareheaded, to put off the shoes, to bend the body, to petition for anything standing, prostrate, kneeling, forms of ceremony, and the like. Now that worship which is always and by all men accounted honourable, may be called natural; the other, which follows places and customs, arbitrary.

12. Furthermore, worship may be enjoined, to wit, by the command of him that is worshipped, and it may be voluntary, namely, such as seems good to the worshipper. If it be enjoined, the actions expressing it do not signify honour, as they signify actions, but as they are enjoined: for they signify obedience immediately, obedience power; insomuch as worship enjoined consists in obedience. Voluntary is honourable only in the nature of the actions, which if they do signify honour to the beholders, it is worship, if not, it is reproach. Again, worship may be either public or private. But public, respecting each single worshipper, may not be voluntary; respecting the city, it may. For seeing that which is done voluntarily, depends on the will of the doer, there would not one worship be given, but as many worships as worshippers, except the will of all men were united by the command of one. But private worship may be voluntary, if it be done secretly; for what is done openly is restrained, either by laws or through modesty, which is contrary to the nature of a voluntary action.

13. Now that we may know what the scope and end of worshipping others is, we must consider the cause why men delight in worship. And we must grant what we have showed elsewhere, that joy consists in this, that a man contemplates virtue, strength, science, beauty, friends, or any power whatsoever, as being, or as though it were his own; and it is nothing

else but a glory or triumph of the mind, conceiving itself honoured, that is to say, loved and feared, that is to say, having the services and assistances of men in readiness. Now because men believe him to be powerful, whom they see honoured, that is to say, esteemed powerful by others, it falls out that honour is increased by worship, and by the opinion of power true power is acquired. His end therefore who either commands or suffers himself to be worshipped, is, that by this means he may acquire as many as he can, either through love or fear, to be obedient unto him.

14. But that we may understand what manner of worship of God natural reason doth assign us, let us begin from his attributes. Where, first, it is manifest that existence is to be allowed him; for there can be no will to honour him, who, we think, hath no being. Next, those philosophers who said, that God was the world, or the world's soul, (that is to say, a part of it) spake unworthily of God; for they attribute nothing to him, but wholly deny his being. For by the word God we understand the world's cause; but in saying that the world is God, they say that it hath no cause, that is as much, as there is no God. In like manner, they who maintain the world not to be created, but eternal; because there can be no cause of an eternal thing, in denying the world to have a cause, they deny also that there is a God. They also have a wretched apprehension of God, who imputing idleness to him, do take from him the government of the world, and of mankind. For, say, they should acknowledge him omnipotent; yet if he mind not these inferior things, that same thread-bare sentence will take place with them: *quod supra nos, nihil ad nos:* what is above us, doth not concern us. And seeing there is nothing for which they should either love or fear him, truly he will be to them as though he were not at all. Moreover, in attributes which signify greatness or power, those which signify some finite or

limited thing, are not signs at all of an honouring mind. For
we honour not God worthily, if we ascribe less power or greatness to him than possibly we can. But every finite thing is less
than we can; for most easily we may always assign and attribute more to a finite thing. No shape therefore must be
assigned to God, for all shape is finite; nor must he be said to
be conceived or comprehended by imagination, or any other
faculty of our soul; for whatsoever we conceive is finite. And
although this word infinite signify a conception of the mind,
yet it follows not that we have any conception of an infinite
thing. For when we say that a thing is infinite, we signify
nothing really, but the impotency in our own mind, as if we
should say, we know not whether or where it is limited. Neither
speak they honourably enough of God, who say we have an
idea of him in our mind; for an idea is our conception, but
conception we have none, except of a finite thing. Nor they,
who say that he hath parts, or that he is some certain entire
thing; which are also attributes of finite things. Nor that he is
in any place; for nothing can be said to be in a place, but what
hath bounds and limits of its greatness on all sides. Nor that
he is moved or is at rest; for either of them suppose a being in
some place. Nor that there are more Gods; because not more
infinites. Furthermore, concerning attributes of happiness, those
are unworthy of God which signify sorrow (unless they be
taken not for any passion, but by a metonomy for the effect)
such as repentance, anger, pity; or want, as appetite, hope,
concupiscence, and that love which is also called lust, for they
are signs of poverty, since it cannot be understood that a man
should desire, hope, and wish for aught, but what he wants
and stands in need of; or any passive faculty, for suffering belongs to a limited power, and which depends upon another.
When we therefore attribute a will to God, it is not to be conceived like unto ours, which is called a rational desire; for if

God desires, he wants, which for any man to say, is a contumely; but we must suppose some resemblance which we cannot conceive. In like manner when we attribute sight and other
acts of the senses to him, or knowledge, or understanding,
which in us are nothing else but a tumult of the mind raised
from outward objects pressing the organs, we must not think
that any such thing befalls the Deity; for it is a sign of power
depending upon some other, which is not the most blessed
thing. He therefore who would not ascribe any other titles to
God than what reason commands, must use such as are either
negative, as infinite, eternal, incomprehensible, &c., or superla-
tive, as most good, most great, most powerful, &c., or indefinite,
as good, just, strong, creator, king, and the like; in such sense,
as not desiring to declare what he is (which were to circum-
scribe him within the narrow limits of our phantasy), but to
confess our own admiration and obedience, which is the property of humility and of a mind yielding all the honour it
possibly can do. For reason dictates one name alone which doth
signify the nature of God, that is, existent, or simply, that he
is; and one in order to, and in relation to us, namely God,
under which is contained both King, and Lord, and Father.

15. Concerning the outward actions wherewith God is to
be worshipped (as also concerning his titles), it is a most general command of reason, that they be signs of a mind yielding
honour. Under which are contained in the first place, prayers.

> Qui fingit sacros auro, vel marmore vultus,
> Non facit ille deos; qui rogat, ille facit.

For prayers are the signs of hope, and hope is an acknowledgment of the divine power or goodness.

In the second place, thanksgiving; which is a sign of the
same affection, but that prayers go before the benefit, and
thanks follow it.

In the third, gifts, that is to say, oblations and sacrifices, for these are thanksgivings.

In the fourth, not to swear by any other. For a man's oath is an imprecation of his wrath against him if he deceive, who both knows whether he do or not, and can punish him if he do, though he be never so powerful; which only belongs to God. For if there were any man from whom his subjects' malice could not lie hid, and whom no human power could resist, plighted faith would suffice without swearing, which, broken, might be punished by that man; and for this very reason there would be no need of an oath.

In the fifth place, to speak warily of God; for that is a sign of fear, and fear is an acknowledgment of power. It follows from this precept, that we may not take the name of God in vain, or use it rashly; for either are inconsiderate. That we must not swear, where there is no need; for that is in vain. But need there is none, unless it be between cities, to avoid or take away contention by force, which necessarily must arise where there is no faith kept in promises, or in a city, for the better certainty of judicature. Also, that we must not dispute of the divine nature; for it is supposed that all things in the natural kingdom of God are inquired into by reason only, that is to say, out of the principles of natural science. But we are so far off by these to attain to the knowledge of the nature of God, that we cannot so much as reach to the full understanding of all the qualities of our own bodies, or of any other creatures. Wherefore there comes nothing from these disputes, but a rash imposition of names to the divine Majesty according to the small measure of our conceptions. It follows also (which belongs to the right of God's kingdom) that their speech is inconsiderate and rash, who say, that this or that doth not stand with divine justice. For even men count it an affront that their children should dispute their right or measure their justice otherwise than by the rule of their commands.

In the sixth, whatsoever is offered up in prayers, thanksgivings, and sacrifices, must in its kind be the best and most betokening honour; namely, prayers must not be rash, or light, or vulgar, but beautiful, and well composed. For though it were absurd in the heathen to worship God in an image, yet was it not against reason to use poetry and music in their churches. Also oblations must be clean, and presents sumptuous, and such as are significative either of submission or gratitude, or commemorative of benefits received; for all these proceed from a desire of honouring.

In the seventh, that God must be worshipped not privately only, but openly and publicly in the sight of all men; because that worship is so much more acceptable, by how much it begets honour and esteem in others (as hath been declared before in art. 13). Unless others therefore see it, that which is most pleasing in our worship vanisheth.

In the last place, that we use our best endeavour to keep the laws of nature. For the undervaluing of our master's command, exceeds all other affronts whatsoever; as on the other side, obedience is more acceptable than all other sacrifices.

And these are principally the natural laws concerning the worship of God; those, I mean, which reason dictates to every man. But to whole cities, every one whereof is one person, the same natural reason further commands an uniformity of public worship. For the actions done by particular persons, according to their private reasons, are not the city's actions, and therefore not the city's worship; but what is done by the city, is understood to be done by the command of him or them who have the sovereignty, wherefore also together with the consent of all the subjects, that is to say, uniformly.

16. The natural laws set down in the foregoing article concerning the divine worship, only command the giving of natural signs of honour. But we must consider that there are two kinds of signs, the one natural, the other done upon agree-

ment, or by express or tacit composition. Now because in every language the use of words and names come by appointment, it may also by appointment be altered; for that which depends on, and derives its force from the will of men, can by the will of the same men agreeing be changed again or abolished. Such names therefore as are attributed to God by the appointment of men, can by the same appointment be taken away. Now what can be done by the appointment of men, that the city may do. The city therefore by right (that is to say, they who have the power of the whole city) shall judge what names or appellations are more, what less honourable for God, that is to say, what doctrines are to be held and professed concerning the nature of God and his operations. Now actions do signify not by men's appointment, but naturally, even as the effects are signs of their causes. Whereof some are always signs of scorn to them before whom they are committed, as those, whereby the body's uncleanness is discovered, and whatsoever men are ashamed to do before those whom they respect; others are always signs of honour, as to draw near and discourse decently and humbly, to give way or to yield in any matter of private benefit. In these actions the city can alter nothing. But there are infinite others, which, as much as belongs to honour or reproach, are indifferent. Now these, by the institution of the city, may both be made signs of honour, and being made so, do in very deed become so. From whence we may understand, that we must obey the city in whatsoever it shall command to be used for a sign of honouring God, that is to say, for worship; provided it can be instituted for a sign of honour, because that is a sign of honour, which by the city's command is used for such.

17. We have already declared which were the laws of God, as well sacred as secular, in his government by the way of nature only. Now because there is no man but may be deceived

in reasoning, and that it so falls out that men are of different opinions concerning the most actions, it may be demanded further, whom God would have to be the interpreter of right reason, that is to say, of his laws. And as for the secular laws, I mean those which concern justice and the carriage of men towards men, by what hath been said before of the constitution of a city, we have demonstratively showed it agreeable to reason, that all judicature belongs to the city, and that judicature is nothing else but an interpretation of the laws, and by consequence, that everywhere cities, that is to say, those who have the sovereign power, are the interpreters of the laws. As for the sacred laws, we must consider what hath been before demonstrated in chap. v. art. 13, that every subject hath transferred as much right as he could on him or them who had the supreme authority. But he could have transferred his right of judging the manner how God is to be honoured, and therefore also he hath done it. That he could, it appears hence, that the manner of honouring God before the constitution of a city was to be fetched from every man's private reason. But every man can subject his private reason to the reason of the whole city. Moreover, if each man should follow his own reason in the worshipping of God, in so great a diversity of worshippers, one would be apt to judge another's worship uncomely, or impious; neither would the one seem to the other to honour God. Even that therefore which were most consonant to reason, would not be a worship, because that the nature of worship consists in this, that it be the sign of inward honour. But there is no sign but whereby somewhat becomes known to others, and therefore is there no sign of honour but what seems so to others. Again, that is a true sign which by the consent of men becomes a sign; therefore also that is honourable, which by the consent of men, that is to say, by the command of the city, becomes a sign of honour. It is not therefore against the will

of God, declared by the way of reason only, to give him such
signs of honour as the city shall command. Wherefore subjects
can transfer their right of judging the manner of God's worship on him or them who have the sovereign power. Nay,
they must do it; for else all manner of absurd opinions concerning the nature of God, and all ridiculous ceremonies which
have been used by any nations, will be seen at once in the
same city. Whence it will fall out, that every man will believe
that all the rest do offer God an affront; so that it cannot be
truly said of any that he worships God; for no man worships
God, that is to say, honours him outwardly, but he who doth
those things, whereby he appears to others for to honour him.
It may therefore be concluded, that the interpretation of all
laws, as well sacred as secular, (God ruling by the way of
nature only), depends on the authority of the city, that is to say,
that man or counsel, to whom the sovereign power is committed; and that whatsoever God commands, he commands by
his voice. And on the other side, that whatsoever is commanded
by them, both concerning the manner of honouring God, and
concerning secular affairs, is commanded by God himself.

18. Against this, some man may demand, first, whether it
doth not follow that the city must be obeyed, if it command us
directly to affront God, or forbid us to worship him? I say, it
does not follow, neither must we obey. For to affront, or not
to worship at all, cannot by any man be understood for a manner of worshipping. Neither also had any one, before the constitution of a city, of those who acknowledge God to rule, a
right to deny him the honour which was then due unto him;
nor could he therefore transfer a right on the city of commanding any such things. Next, if it be demanded whether the
city must be obeyed if it command somewhat to be said or
done, which is not a disgrace to God directly, but from whence
by reasoning disgraceful consequences may be derived: as for

example, if it were commanded to worship God in an image, before those who account that honourable: truly it is to be done.* For worship is instituted in sign of honour; but to worship him thus, is a sign of honour, and increaseth God's honour among those who do so account of it. Or if it be commanded to call God by a name which we know not what it signifies, or how it can agree with this word God; that also must be done. For what we do for honour's sake, (and we know no better), if it be taken for a sign of honour, it is a sign of honour; and therefore if we refuse to do it, we refuse the enlarging of God's honour. The same judgment must be had of all the attributes and actions about the merely rational worship of God, which may be controverted and disputed. For though this kind of commands may be sometimes contrary to right reason, and therefore sins in them who command them; yet are they not against right reason, nor sins in subjects, whose right reason in points of controversy is that, which submits itself to the reason of the city. Lastly, if that man or counsel who hath the supreme power, command himself to be worshipped with the same attributes and actions, wherewith God is to be worshipped, the question is, whether we must obey.

* We said in art. 14 of this chapter, that they who attributed limits to God, transgressed the natural law concerning God's worship. Now they who worship him in an image, assign him limits. Wherefore they do that which they ought not to do, and this place seems to contradict the former. We must therefore know first, that they who are constrained by authority, do not set God any bounds, but they who command them. For they who worship unwillingly, do worship in very deed; but they either stand or fall there, where they are commanded to stand or fall by a lawful sovereign. Secondly, I say it must be done, not at all times and everywhere, but on supposition that there is no other rule of worshipping God beside the dictates of human reason; for then the will of the city stands for reason. But in the kingdom of God by way of covenant, whether old or new, where idolatry is expressly forbid, though the city commands us to worship thus, yet must we not do it. Which, if he shall consider, who conceived some repugnancy between this and art. 14, will surely cease to think so any longer.

There are many things, which may be commonly attributed both to God and men; for even men may be praised and magnified. And there are many actions, whereby God and men may be worshipped. But the significations of the attributes and actions are only to be regarded. Those attributes therefore, whereby we signify ourselves to be of an opinion, that there is any man endued with a sovereignty independent from God, or that he is immortal, or of infinite power, and the like, though commanded by princes, yet must they be abstained from. As also from those actions signifying the same, as prayer to the absent; to ask those things which God alone can give, as rain and fair weather; to offer him what God can only accept, as oblations, holocausts; or to give a worship, than which a greater cannot be given, as sacrifice. For these things seem to tend to this end, that God may not be thought to rule, contrary to what was supposed from the beginning. But genuflection, prostration, or any other act of the body whatsoever, may be lawfully used even in civil worship; for they may signify an acknowledgment of the civil power only. For divine worship is distinguished from civil, not by the motion, placing, habit, or gesture of the body, but by the declaration of our opinion of him whom we do worship. As if we cast down ourselves before any man, with intention of declaring by that sign that we esteem him as God, it is divine worship; if we do the same thing as a sign of our acknowledgment of the civil power, it is civil worship. Neither is the divine worship distinguished from civil, by any action usually understood by the words λατρεία and δουλεία, whereof the former marking out the duty of servants, the latter their destiny, they are words of the same action in degree.

19. From what hath been said may be gathered, that God reigning by the way of natural reason only, subjects do sin, first, if they break the moral laws, which are unfolded in chap-

ters II. and III. Secondly, if they break the laws or commands
of the city in those things which pertain to justice. Thirdly, if
they worship not God κατὰ τὰ νόμικα. Fourthly, if they
confess not before men, both in words and deeds, that there is
one God most good, most great, most blessed, the Supreme King
of the world and of all worldly kings; that is to say, if they do
not worship God. This fourth sin in the natural kingdom of
God, by what hath been said in the foregoing chapter in art. 2,
is the sin of treason against the Divine Majesty. For it is a
denying of the Divine Power, or atheism. For sins proceed here,
just as if we should suppose some man to be the sovereign
king, who being himself absent, should rule by his viceroy.
Against whom sure they would transgress, who should not
obey his viceroy in all things; except he usurped the kingdom
to himself, or would give it to some other, but they who should
so absolutely obey him, as not to admit of this exception, might
be said to be guilty of treason.

Chapter XVI

Of the Kingdom of God under the Old Covenant

(The text of this chapter is omitted.)

Chapter XVII

Of the Kingdom of God by the New Covenant

(The text of this chapter is omitted.)

Chapter XVIII

Concerning Those Things Which Are Necessary for Our Entrance into the Kingdom of Heaven

1. It was ever granted, that all authority in secular matters derived from him who had the sovereign power, whether he were one man or an assembly of men. That the same in spiritual matters depended on the authority of the Church, is manifest by the lastly foregoing proofs; and besides by this, that all Christian cities are Churches endued with this kind of authority. From whence a man, though but dull of apprehension, may collect, that in a Christian city (that is to say, in a city whose sovereignty belongs to a Christian prince or council) all power, as well spiritual as secular, is united under Christ, and therefore it is to be obeyed in all things. But on the other side, because we must rather obey God than men, there is a difficulty risen, how obedience may safely be yielded to them, if at any time somewhat should be commanded by them to be done which Christ hath prohibited. The reason of this difficulty is, that seeing God no longer speaks to us by Christ and his prophets in open voice, but by the holy Scriptures, which by divers men are diversely understood, they know indeed what princes and a congregated Church do command, but whether that which they do command, be contrary to the word of God or not, this they know not; but with a wavering obedience between the punishments of temporal and spiritual death, as it were sailing between Scylla and Charybdis, they often run themselves upon both. But they who rightly distinguish between the things necessary to salvation, and those which are

not necessary, can have none of this kind of doubt. For if the command of the prince or city be such, that he can obey it without hazard of his eternal salvation, it is unjust not to obey them; and the apostle's precepts take place (Col. iii. 20,22): *Children obey your parents in all things: servants in all things obey your masters according to the flesh.* And the command of Christ (Matth. xxiii. 2-3): *The Scribes and Pharisees sit in Moses' chair; all things therefore whatsoever they command you, that observe and do.* On the contrary, if they command us to do those things which are punished with eternal death, it were madness not rather to choose to die a natural death, than by obeying to die eternally; and then comes in that which Christ says (Matth. x. 28): *Fear not them who kill the body, but cannot kill the soul.* We must see therefore what all those things are, which are necessary to salvation.

2. Now all things necessary to salvation are comprehended in two virtues, faith and obedience, the latter of these, if it could be perfect, would alone suffice to preserve us from damnation; but because we have all of us been long since guilty of disobedience against God in Adam, and besides we ourselves have since actually sinned, obedience is not sufficient without remission of sins. But this, together with our entrance into the kingdom of heaven, is the reward of faith; nothing else is requisite to salvation. For the kingdom of heaven is shut to none but sinners, that is to say, those who have not performed due obedience to the laws; and not to those neither, if they believe the necessary articles of the Christian faith. Now, if we shall know in what points obedience doth consist, and which are the necessary articles of the Christian faith, it will at once be manifest what we must do, and what abstain from, at the command of cities and of princes.

3. But by obedience in this place is signified not the fact, but the will and desire wherewith we purpose and endeavour

as much as we can to obey for the future. In which sense the word obedience is equivalent to repentance; for the virtue of repentance consists not in the sorrow which accompanies the remembrance of sin, but in our conversion into the way, and full purpose to sin no more; without which that sorrow is said to be the sorrow not of a penitent, but a desperate person. But because they who love God cannot but desire to obey the divine law, and they who love their neighbours cannot but desire to obey the moral law, which consists as hath been showed above in chap. III. in the prohibition of pride, ingratitude, contumely, inhumanity, cruelty, injury, and the like offences, whereby our neighbours are prejudiced, therefore also love or charity is equivalent to obedience. Justice also (which is a constant will of giving to every man his due) is equivalent with it. But that faith and repentance are sufficient for salvation, is manifest by the covenant itself of baptism. For they who were by Peter converted on the day of Pentecost, demanding him, what they should do, he answered (Acts ii. 38): *Repent and be baptized every one of you in the name of Jesus for the remission of your sins.* There was nothing therefore to be done for the obtaining of baptism, that is to say, for to enter into the kingdom of God, but to repent and believe in the name of Jesus; for the kingdom of heaven is promised by the covenant which is made in baptism. Furthermore, by the words of Christ, answering the lawyer who asked him what he should do to inherit eternal life (Luke xviii. 20): *Thou knowest the commandments: Thou shalt not kill, thou shalt not commit adultery,* &c., which refer to obedience, and (Mark x. 21): *Sell all that thou hast, and come and follow me,* which relates to faith. And by that which is said: *The just shall live by faith,* (not every man, but the just); for justice is the same disposition of will which repentance and obedience are. And by the words of St. Mark (i. 15): *The time is fulfilled, and the kingdom of*

God is at hand; repent ye, and believe the gospel, by which
words is not obscurely signified that there is no need of other
virtues for our entrance into the kingdom of God, excepting
those of repentance and faith. The obedience therefore which
is necessarily required to salvation, is nothing else but the will
or endeavour to obey, that is to say, of doing according to the
laws of God, that is, the moral laws, which are the same to all
men, and the civil laws, that is to say, the commands of sovereigns in temporal matters, and the ecclesiastical laws in spiritual; which two kinds of laws are divers in divers cities and
Churches, and are known by their promulgation and public
sentences.

4. That we may understand what the Christian faith is, we
must define faith in general, and distinguish it from those
other acts of the mind wherewith commonly it is confounded.
The object of faith universally taken, namely, for that which
is believed, is evermore a proposition, (that is to say, a speech
affirmative or negative) which we grant to be true. But because
propositions are granted for divers causes, it falls out, that this
kind of concessions are diversely called. But we grant propositions sometimes, which notwithstanding we receive not into our
minds; and this either for a time, to wit, so long, till by consideration of the consequences, we have well examined the truth
of them, which we call supposing; or also simply, as through
fear of the laws, which is to profess, or confess by outward
tokens; or for a voluntary compliance sake, which men use out
of civility to those whom they respect, and for love of peace
to others, which is absolute yielding. Now the propositions
which we receive for truth, we always grant for some reasons
of our own; and these are derived either from the proposition
itself, or from the person propounding. They are derived from
the proposition itself, by calling to mind what things those
words which make up the proposition do by common consent

usually signify. If so, then the assent which we give, is called knowledge or science. But if we cannot remember what is certainly understood by those words, but sometimes one thing, sometimes another seem to be apprehended by us, then we are said to think. For example, if it be propounded that two and three make five; and by calling to mind the order of those numeral words, that it is so appointed by the common consent of them who are of the same language with us, (as it were by a certain contract necessary for human society), that five shall be the name of so many unities as are contained in two and three taken together, a man assents that this is therefore true because two and three together are the same with five: this assent shall be called knowledge, and to know this truth is nothing else but to acknowledge that it is made by ourselves. For by whose will and rules of speaking the number | | is called two, | | | is called three, and | | | | | is called five, by their will also it comes to pass that this proposition is true, two and three taken together make five. In like manner if we remember what it is that is called theft, and what injury, we shall understand by the words themselves, whether it be true that theft is an injury, or not. Truth is the same with a true proposition; but the proposition is true in which the word consequent, which by logicians is called the predicate, embraceth the word antecedent in its amplitude, which they call the subject. And to know truth, is the same thing as to remember that it was made by ourselves by the common use of words. Neither was it rashly nor unadvisedly said by Plato of old, that knowledge was memory. But it happens sometimes that words although they have a certain and defined signification by constitution, yet by vulgar use either to adorn or deceive, they are so wrested from their own significations, that to remember the conceptions for which they were first imposed on things is very hard, and not to be mastered but by a sharp

judgment and very great diligence. It happens too, that there
are many words which have no proper, determined, and everywhere the same signification; and are understood not by their
own, but by virtue of other signs used together with them.
Thirdly, there are some words of things unconceivable. Of those
things therefore whereof they are the words, there is no conception; and therefore in vain do we seek for the truth of those
propositions, which they make out of the words themselves. In
these cases, while by considering the definitions of words we
search out the truth of some proposition, according to the hope
we have of finding it, we think it sometimes true, and sometimes false; either of which apart is called thinking, and also
believing; both together, doubting. But when our reasons for
which we assent to some proposition, derive not from the
proposition itself, but from the person propounding, whom we
esteem so learned that he is not deceived, and we see no reason
why he should deceive us, our assent, because it grows not
from any confidence of our own, but from another man's
knowledge, is called faith. And by the confidence of whom we
do believe, we are said to trust them, or to trust in them. By
what hath been said, the difference appears, first, between faith
and profession; for that is always joined with inward assent,
this not always. That is an inward persuasion of the mind, this
an outward obedience. Next, between faith and opinion; for
this depends on our own reason, that on the good esteem we
have of another. Lastly, between faith and knowledge; for this
deliberately takes a proposition broken and chewed; that swal-
lows it down whole and entire. The explication of words,
whereby the matter enquired after is propounded, is conducible
to knowledge; nay, the only way to know, is by definition.
But this is prejudicial to faith; for those things which exceed
human capacity, and are propounded to be believed, are never
more evident by explication, but on the contrary more obscure,

and harder to be credited. And the same thing befalls a man, who endeavours to demonstrate the mysteries of faith by natural reason, which happens to a sick man, who will needs chew before he will swallow his wholesome but bitter pills; whence it comes to pass, that he presently brings them up again, which perhaps would otherwise, if he had taken them well down, have proved his remedy.

5. We have seen therefore what it is to believe. But what is it to believe in Christ? Or what proposition is that which is the object of our faith in Christ? For when we say, I believe in Christ, we signify indeed whom, but not what we believe. Now, to believe in Christ is nothing else but to believe that Jesus is the Christ, namely he, who according to the prophecies of Moses and the prophets of Israel, was to come into this world to institute the kingdom of God. And this sufficiently appears out of the words of Christ himself to Martha (John xi. 25-27): *I am*, saith he, *the resurrection and the life; he that believeth in me, though he were dead, yet shall he live; and whosoever liveth and believeth in me, shall never die. Believest thou this? She saith unto him, Yea, Lord, I believe that thou art the Christ the Son of God, which should come into the world.* In which words, we see that the question, *believest thou in me?* is expounded by the answer, *thou art the Christ.* To believe in Christ therefore is nothing else but to believe Jesus himself, saying that he is the Christ.

6. Faith and obedience both necessarily concurring to salvation, what kind of obedience that same is, and to whom due, hath been showed above in art. 3. But now we must enquire what articles of faith are requisite. And I say, that to a Christion* there is no other article of faith requisite as necessary

---

* Although I conceive this assertion to be sufficiently proved by the following reasons, yet I thought it worth my labour to make a more ample explication of it, because I perceive that being somewhat new, it may pos-

to salvation, but only this, that Jesus is the Christ. But we must
distinguish (as we have already done before in art. 4) between
faith and profession. A profession therefore, of more articles
(if they be commanded) may be necessary; for it is a part of
our obedience due to the laws. But we enquire not now what
obedience, but what faith, is necessary to salvation. And this is

---

sibly be distasteful to many divines. First therefore, when I say this
article, that Jesus is the Christ, is necessary to salvation; I say not that
faith only is necessary, but I require justice also, or that obedience which
is due to the laws of God, that is to say, a will to live righteously.
Secondly, I deny not but the profession of many articles, (provided that
that profession be commanded by the Church) is also necessary to salvation. But seeing faith is internal, profession external, I say that the former
only is properly faith; the latter a part of obedience; insomuch as that
article alone sufficeth for inward belief, but is not sufficient for the outward profession of a Christian. Lastly, even as if I had said that true
and inward repentance of sins was only necessary to salvation, yet were
it not to be held for a paradox, because we suppose justice, obedience, and
a mind reformed in all manner of virtues to be contained in it. So when
I say that the faith of one article is sufficient to salvation, it may well
be less wondered at, seeing that in it so many other articles are contained.
For these words, Jesus is the Christ, do signify that Jesus was that
person, whom God had promised by his prophets should come into the
world to establish his kingdom; that is to say, that Jesus is the Son of
God, the creator of heaven and earth, born of a virgin, dying for the
sins of them who should believe in him; that he was Christ, that is to
say, a king; that he revived (for else he were not like to reign) to judge
the world, and to reward every one according to his works, for otherwise he cannot be a king; also that men shall rise again, for otherwise
they are not like to come to judgment. The whole symbol of the apostles
is therefore contained in this one article; which, notwithstanding, I
thought reasonable to contract thus, because I found that many men
for this alone, without the rest, were admitted into the kingdom of God,
both by Christ and his apostles; as the thief on the cross, the eunuch
baptized by Philip, the two thousand men converted to the Church at
once by St. Peter. But if any man be displeased that I do not judge all
those eternally damned, who do not inwardly assent to every article
defined by the Church (and yet do not contradict, but, if they be commanded, do submit), I know not what I shall say to them. For the most
evident testimonies of Holy Writ, which do follow, do withhold me from
altering my opinion.

proved, first, out of the scope of the Evangelists, which was by
the description of our Saviour's life to establish this one article;
and we shall know that such was the scope and counsel of the
Evangelists, if we observe but the history itself. St. Matthew
(chap. i.), beginning at this genealogy, shows that Jesus was of
the lineage of David, born of a virgin; (chap. ii.) that he was
adored by the wise men as king of the Jews; that Herod for
the same cause sought to slay him; (chap. iii., iv.) that his
kingdom was preached both by John the Baptist and himself;
(chapters v., vi., vii.) that he taught the laws, not as the Scribes,
but as one having authority; (chapters viii., ix.) that he cured
diseases miraculously; (chap. x.) that he sent his apostles, the
preachers of his kingdom, throughout all the parts of Judea
to proclaim his kingdom; (chap. xi.) that he commanded the
messengers, sent from John to enquire whether he were the
Christ or not, to tell him what they had seen, namely,
the miracles which were only compatible with Christ; (chap.
xii.) that he proved and declared his kingdom to the Pharisees
and others by arguments, parables, and signs; and (the following chapters to xxi.) that he maintained himself to be the Christ
against the Pharisees; (chap. xxi.) that he was saluted with
the title of king, when he entered into Jerusalem; (chaps. xxii.,
xxiii., xxiv., xxv.) that he forewarned others of false Christs;
and that he showed in parables what manner of kingdom his
should be; (chaps. xxvi., xxvii.) that he was taken and accused
for this reason, because he said he was a king; and that a title
was written on his cross, *this is Jesus the king of the Jews;* lastly,
(chap. xxviii.) that after his resurrection, he told his apostles
that all power was given unto him both in heaven and in
earth. All which tends to this end, that we should believe Jesus
to be the Christ. Such therefore was the scope of St. Matthew
in describing his gospel. But such as his was, such also was
the rest of the Evangelists; which St. John sets down expressly

in the end of his gospel (John xx. 31): *These things,* saith he, *are written, that ye may know that Jesus is the Christ, the Son of the living God.*

7. Secondly, this is proved by the preaching of the apostles. For they were the proclaimers of his kingdom; neither did Christ send them to preach aught but the kingdom of God (Luke ix. 2; Acts x. 42). And what they did after Christ his ascension, may be understood by the accusation which was brought against them (Acts xvii. 6-7): *They drew Jason,* saith St. Luke, *and certain brethren unto the rulers of the city, crying, These are the men that have turned the world upside down, and are come hither also, whom Jason hath received; and these all do contrary to the decrees of Cæsar, saying that there is another king, one Jesus.* It appears also what the subject of the apostle's sermons was, out of these words (Acts xvii. 2-3): *Opening and alleging out of the Scriptures* (to wit, of the Old Testament) *that Christ must needs have suffered, and risen again from the dead, and that this Jesus is the Christ.*

8. Thirdly, by the places in which the easiness of those things which are required by Christ to the attaining of salvation, is declared. For if an internal assent of the mind were necessarily required to the truth of all and each proposition which this day is controverted about the Christian faith, or by divers churches is diversely defined, there would be nothing more difficult than the Christian religion. And how then would that be true (Matth. xi. 30): *My yoke is easy and my burden light;* and that (Matth. xviii. 6): *Little ones do believe in him;* and that (1 Cor. i. 21): *It pleased God by the foolishness of preaching, to save those that believe?* Or how was the thief hanging on the cross sufficiently instructed to salvation, the confession of whose faith was contained in these words: *Lord, remember me when thou comest into thy kingdom?* Or how

could St. Paul himself, from an enemy, so soon become a doctor of Christians?

9. Fourthly, by this, that that article is the foundation of faith, neither rests it on any other foundation. Matth. xxiv. 23, 24: *If any man shall say unto you, Lo here is Christ, or he is there, believe it not; for there shall arise false Christs and false prophets, and shall show great signs and wonders,* &c. Whence it follows, that for the faith's sake which we have in this article, we must not believe any signs and wonders. Gal. i. 8: *Although we or an angel from heaven,* saith the apostle, *should preach to you any other gospel, than what we have preached, let him be accursed.* By reason of this article, therefore, we might not trust the very apostles and angels themselves (and therefore, I conceive, not the Church neither) if they should teach the contrary. 1 John iv. 1-2: *Beloved, believe not every spirit, but try the spirits whether they are of God, because many false prophets are gone out into the world. Hereby know ye the spirit of God; every spirit that confesseth Jesus Christ is come in the flesh, is of God,* &c. That article therefore is the measure of the spirits, whereby the authority of the doctors is either received, or rejected. It cannot be denied, indeed, but that all who at this day are Christians, did learn from the doctors, that it was Jesus who did all those things whereby he might be acknowledged to be the Christ. Yet it follows not, that the same persons believed that article for the doctors' or the Church's, but for Jesus' his own sake. For that article was before the Christian Church, (Matth. xvi. 18), although all the rest were after it; and the Church was founded upon it, not it upon the Church. Besides, this article, that Jesus is the Christ, is so fundamental, that all the rest are by St. Paul said to be built upon it (I Cor. iii, 11-15): *For other foundation can no man lay, than that which is laid, which is Jesus Christ* (that is to say, that Jesus is the Christ). *Now if*

any man build upon this foundation, gold, silver, precious
stones, wood, hay, stubble, every man's work shall be made
manifest; if any man's work abide which he hath built there-
upon, he shall receive a reward; if any man's work shall be
burnt, he shall suffer loss, but he himself shall be saved. From
whence it plainly appears, that by foundation is understood this
article, that Jesus is the Christ: for gold, and silver, precious
stones, wood, hay, stubble (whereby the doctrines are signified)
are not built upon the person of Christ; and also, that false
doctrines may be raised upon this foundation, yet not so, as they
must necessarily be damned who teach them.

10. Lastly, that this article alone is needful to be inwardly
believed, may be most evidently proved out of many places
of holy Scripture, let who will be the interpreter. John v. 39:
Search the Scriptures, for in them ye think ye have eternal
life; and they are they which testify of me. But Christ meant
the Scriptures of the Old Testament only; for the New was
then not yet written. Now, there is no other testimony concerning Christ in the Old Testament, but that an eternal king
was to come in such a place, that he was to be born of such
parents, that he was to teach and do such things, whereby, as
by certain signs, he was to be known. All which testify this
one thing, that Jesus who was so born, and did teach and do
such things, was the Christ. Other faith then was not required
to attain eternal life, besides this article, John xi. 26: *Whoso-*
ever liveth and believeth in me, shall never die. But to believe
in Jesus (as is there expressed) is the same with believing that
Jesus was the Christ. He therefore that believes that, shall
never die; and by consequence, that article alone is necessary
to salvation. John xx. 31: *These are written, that ye might be-*
lieve that Jesus is the Christ, the Son of God; and that believ-
ing, ye might have life through his name. Wherefore he that
believes thus, shall have eternal life, and therefore needs no

other faith. 1 John iv. 2: *Every spirit, that confesseth that Jesus Christ is come in the flesh, is of God.* And 1 John v. 1: *Whosoever believeth that Jesus is the Christ, is born of God.* And 1 John v. 5: *Who is he that overcometh the world, but he that believeth that Jesus is the Son of God?* If therefore there be no need to believe anything else, to the end a man may be of God, born of God, and overcome the world, than that Jesus is the Christ; that one article then is sufficient to salvation. Acts viii. 36-37: *See, here is water; what doth hinder me to be baptized? And Philip said, If thou believest with all thine heart, thou mayest. And he answered and said, I believe that Jesus Christ is the Son of God.* If then this article being believed with the whole heart (that is to say, with inward faith) was sufficient for baptism, it is also sufficient for salvation. Besides these places, there are innumerable others, which do clearly and expressly affirm the same thing. Nay, wheresoever we read that our Saviour commended the faith of any one, or that he said, thy faith hath saved thee, or that he healed any one for his faith's sake, there the proposition believed was no other but this, Jesus is the Christ, either directly or consequently.

11. But because no man can believe Jesus to be the Christ, who, when he knows that by Christ is understood that same king who was promised from God by Moses and the prophets, for to be the king and Saviour of the world, doth not also believe Moses and the prophets; neither can he believe these, who believes not that God is, and that he governs the world; it is necessary, that the faith of God and of the Old Testament be contained in this faith of the New. Seeing therefore that atheism, and the denial of the Divine Providence, were the only treason against the Divine Majesty in the kingdom of God by nature, but idolatry also in the kingdom of God by the old covenant; now in this kingdom wherein God rules by way of a new covenant, apostasy is also added, or the re-

nunciation of this article once received, that Jesus is the Christ. Truly other doctrines, provided they have their determination from a lawful Church, are not to be contradicted; for that is the sin of disobedience. But it hath been fully declared before, that they are not needful to be believed with an inward faith.

12. Faith and obedience have divers parts in accomplishing the salvation of a Christian; for this contributes the power or capacity, that, the act; and either is said to justify in its kind. For Christ forgives not the sins of all men, but of the penitent or the obedient, that is to say, the just. I say not the guiltless, but the just; for justice is a will of obeying the laws, and may be consistent with a sinner; and with Christ, the will to obey is obedience. For not every man, but the just shall live by faith. Obedience therefore justifies, because it maketh just in the same manner as temperance maketh temperate, prudence prudent, chastity chaste, namely, essentially; and puts a man in such a state, as makes him capable of pardon. Again, Christ hath not promised forgiveness of sins to all just men, but only those of them who believe him to be the Christ. Faith therefore justifies in such a sense as a judge may be said to justify, who absolves, namely, by the sentence which actually saves a man; and in this acception of justification (for it is an equivocal term) faith alone justifies, but in the other, obedience only. But neither obedience alone, nor faith alone, do save us, but both together.

13. By what hath been said hitherto, it will be easy to discern what the duty of Christian subjects is towards their sovereigns, who, as long as they profess themselves Christians, cannot command their subjects to deny Christ, or to offer him any contumely; for if they should command this, they would profess themselves to be no Christians. For seeing we have showed, both by natural reason and out of holy Scriptures, that subjects ought in all things to obey their princes and gov-

ernors, excepting those which are contrary to the command of
God; and that the commands of God, in a Christian city, concerning temporal affairs, (that is to say, those which are to be
discussed by human reason) are the laws and sentence of the
city, delivered from those who have received authority from
the city to make laws and judge of controversies; but concerning spiritual matters, (that is to say, those which are to be
defined by the holy Scripture) are the laws and sentences of
the city, that is to say, the Church, (for a Christian city and a
Church, as hath been showed in the foregoing chapter, art. 10,
are the same thing), delivered by pastors lawfully ordained,
and who have to that end authority given them by the city; it
manifestly follows, that in a Christian commonweal, obedience
is due to the sovereign in all things, as well spiritual as temporal. And that the same obedience, even from a Christian
subject, is due in all temporal matters to those princes who are
no Christians, is without any controversy; but in matters spiritual, that is to say, those things which concern God's worship,
some Christian Church is to be followed. For it is an hypothesis
of the Christian faith, that God speaks not in things supernatural, but by the way of Christian interpreters of holy Scriptures. But what? Must we resist princes, when we cannot obey
them? Truly, no; for this is contrary to our civil covenant.
What must we do then? Go to Christ by martyrdom; which
if it seem to any man to be a hard saying, most certain it is
that he believes not with his whole heart, that Jesus is the
Christ, the Son of the living God (for he would then desire
to be dissolved, and to be with Christ), but he would by a
feigned Christian faith elude that obedience which he hath
contracted to yield unto the city.

14. But some men perhaps will wonder, if (excepting this
one article, that Jesus is the Christ, which only is necessary to
salvation in relation to internal faith) all the rest belong to

obedience, which may be performed, although a man do not inwardly believe, (so he do but desire to believe, and make an outward profession, as oft as need requires, of whatsoever is propounded by the Church), how it comes about that there are so many tenets, which are all held so to concern our faith, that except a man do inwardly believe them, he cannot enter into the kingdom of heaven. But if he consider that in most con-troversies the contention is about human sovereignty; in some, matter of gain and profit; in others, the glory of wits; he will surely wonder the less. The question about the propriety of the Church, is a question about the right of sovereignty. For it being known what a Church is, it is known at once to whom the rule over Christians doth belong. For if every Christian city be that Church which Christ himself hath commanded every Christian, subject to that city, to hear, then every subject is bound to obey his city, that is to say, him or them who have the supreme power, not only in temporal, but also in spiritual matters. But if every Christian city be not that Church, then is there some other Church more universal, which must be obeyed. All Christians therefore must obey that Church just as they would obey Christ if he came upon earth. She will therefore rule, either by the way of monarchy, or by some as-sembly. This question then concerns the right of ruling. To the same end belongs the question concerning infallibility; for whosoever were truly and internally believed by all mankind, that he could not err, would be sure of all dominion, as well temporal as spiritual, over all mankind, unless himself would refuse it. For if he say that he must be obeyed in temporals because it is supposed he cannot err, that right of dominion is immediately granted him. Hither also tends the privilege of interpreting Scriptures. For he to whom it belongs to interpret the controversies arising from the divers interpretations of Scrip-tures, hath authority also simply and absolutely to determine all manner of controversies whatsoever. But he who hath this, hath also the command over all men who acknowledge the Scriptures to be the word of God. To this end drive all the disputes about the power of remitting, and retaining sins; or the authority of excommunication. For every man, if he be in his wits, will in all things yield that man an absolute obedience, by virtue of whose sentence he believes himself to be either saved, or damned. Hither also tends the power of instituting societies; for they depend on him by whom they subsist, who hath as many subjects as monks, although living in an enemy's city. To this end also refers the question concerning the judge of lawful matrimony; for he to whom that judicature belongs, to him also pertains the knowledge of all those cases which concern the inheritance and succession of all the goods and rights, not of private men only, but also of sovereign princes. And hither also in some respect tends the virgin life of ecclesiastical persons; for unmarried men have less coherence than others with civil society. And besides, it is an inconvenience not to be slighted, that princes must either necessarily forego the priesthood (which is a great bond of civil obedience) or have no hereditary kingdom. To this end also tends the canonization of saints, which the heathen called apotheosis; for he that can allure foreign subjects with so great a reward, may bring those who are greedy of such glory, to dare and do anything. For what was it but an honourable name with posterity, which the Decii and other Romans sought after, and a thousand others, who cast themselves upon incredible perils? The controversies about purgatory, and indulgences, are matter of gain. The questions of free-will, justification, and the manner of receiving Christ in the sacrament, are philosophical. There are also questions concerning some rites not introduced, but left in the Church not sufficiently purged from Gentilism. But we need reckon no more. All the world knows that such is the nature of men, that dissenting in questions which concern their power, or profit, or pre-eminence of wit, they slander and curse each other. It is not therefore to be wondered at, if almost all tenets (after men grew hot with disputings) are held forth by some or other to be necessary to salvation and for our entrance into the kingdom of heaven. Insomuch as they who hold them not, are not only condemned as guilty of disobedience (which in truth they are, after the Church hath once defined them) but of infidelity, which I have declared above to be wrong, out of many evident places of Scripture. To which I add this one of Saint Paul's (Rom. xiv. 3, 5): *Let not him that eateth, despise him that eateth not, and let not him that eateth not, judge him that eateth; for God hath received him. One man esteemeth one day above another, another esteemeth every day alike. Let every man be fully persuaded in his own mind.*

(1)